The Christian Revolutionary

BY

MARK ALLEN LUDWIG

Lexington & Concord Partners, Ltd.
PO Box 5106
Balboa, Ancon
Panama City 800, Panama
First English Edition
—2001—

1 2 3 4 5 6 7 8 9 10 11 12 13 14 15

"For the statutes of Omri are kept, and all the works of the house of Ahab, and ye walk in their counsels, that I should make thee a desolation"—Micah 6:16

"Cursed be the man that trusteth in man, and maketh flesh his arm, and whose heart departeth from Yahweh."
—Jeremiah 17:5

Contents

The Christian Revolutionary

CHAPTER 1
The Failure of Good Men

Anyone who has been concerned with the moral decline of their nation in recent years cannot help but notice that one common thread winds its way through every effort to reform and change the direction we are headed. That common thread is *failure*. Whatever the issue or the cause, no matter the strategy employed, no matter who is involved or where, the best that ever seems to be achieved is a certain tenuous holding on, and that only with great effort and expense. Victories are few and temporary. Defeats are effectively irreversible.

The thinking man has to wonder at this fact. To be defeated once, or even several times, might be brushed aside as tactical error. To be continually defeated for decades together on every front speaks of a deeper failure. Many blame a hostile media, or powerful interests in government, or well-heeled opponents. Few indeed have been willing to take the blame themselves. Yet in the last analysis, that is where it belongs. A commander of an army who cannot win battles will be relieved of his command, either by his superiors or by a victorious enemy. If his strategy doesn't work, he must change it. When he doesn't wake up and face reality—and change accordingly—he *deserves* to be blamed.

Yet if this is the case, what does the future hold? Unless something changes drastically, tyranny is going to triumph, lies are going to triumph, and a darkness unimagined since the beginning of human history will descend upon us and our children. Anyone who has a sense of history—even if only in the twentieth century—can appreciate the depths to which man can descend, and how fast he can do it. Likewise, anyone who has had a taste of modern technology can well extrapolate how man could descend to a far greater depth of darkness than he ever has in the past.

Make no mistake, the modern state is going to be driven to use everything it can to insure its survival in the coming generation. That is due to the simple fact that technology has fundamentally altered the power equation that the modern state is based on. Modern representative government is based on an eighteenth century theory of power: that power resides in the people, and specifically in large numbers, or majorities. In the eighteenth century that was true. For example, in the context of a military conflict, the biggest army generally won. An army might use its numbers more effectively with a clever strategy, but the ten-to-one size advantage was hard to beat. Today that is not necessarily the case. One man with a biological toxin can now wreak more havoc in a city in two days than a large army of two hundred years ago could in two months.

Modern governments are fundamentally incapable of dealing with this power shift. They are designed to accommodate majorities and significant minorities, not small but powerful minorities (a single individual being the ultimate minority). Simply put, they give the majority the right to legislate, and demand that minorities submit to the majority's will as expressed in legislation. A hundred years ago such a demand only conformed to the irresistible power equation behind the state. Today, the minority has other options.

This situation presents a fundamental challenge to the state. Unless the state meets that challenge it will be destroyed. The primary resource that modern nations are using to meet this challenge is brute force. This, in turn, is driving the modern state on an accelerating spiral toward a mind-boggling totalitarianism. At bottom, the state has too much philosophical baggage to ever accommodate a minority that cannot somehow ingratiate itself with the nation's rulers. It will always justify the majority and condemn the recalcitrant minority as criminal. And in the end, the state will do anything to survive. The majority will drive it to because anything is more tolerable than anarchy and terror in every quarter.

A state subject to such pressures will destroy personal freedoms, including all religious liberty and the freedom of thought and expression. It must. In a world where a single act by a single disgruntled individual could kill millions and threaten both the fabric of society and the viability of the state, the state must work toward making such criminal acts simply impossible in the first place. Secondly, it must work to stop crimes before they happen, while they are still just thoughts. To accomplish this, the state must first of all destroy all competing loyalties. Man must become a creature of the state, whose very being is wrapped up in the state, and therefore he cannot think beyond it or against it in any meaningful way. Religion and family are the two strongest competing loyalties, and so must be done away with.

We should pause to consider well where all of this leads because, unless something changes, it is *our* future. Religiously speaking, we're almost living in this future already. The great churches of our day preach a "broad gate" religion that accommodates a social morality and upholds the state in its claims over our lives. Such churches are leading multitudes into hell and they know it not. The dissenters from this social religion are being stigmatized as dangerous fanatics. They will eventually be co-opted or outlawed.

Likewise, the family is also in a state of collapse. It will—and must—be taken further into oblivion though. The ancient dream of the philosophers of dissolving the family entirely is at our doorstep. When children are being raised badly, when they're not coping well, committing suicide, becoming dependent on drugs (legal and illegal) and going berserk, there does come a time when it is valid to argue that children would be better off raised by competent professionals rather than dysfunctional parents. It is already technologically possible to separate human reproduction from sexuality, and vice versa. Sperm and egg banks already exist. *In vitro* fertilization is routine. Children can be conceived, brought to viability and raised entirely by competent experts outside the context of sexual union and family. Such children would have no identity apart from the state. Effectively parentless, they could be raised according to state guidelines for state purposes without hindrance. If they developed problems, their professional surrogate parents would routinely and unemotionally expose these problems early on so they could be appropriately dealt with.

If this were not bad enough, the need to catch crimes in the conceptual stage will drive the state to work towards a sort of continuous computerized psychoanalysis of the entire population. Such analysis is already being done on financial transactions in Europe by Interpol, and in the United States by Fincen. This kind of analysis is essentially an attempt to discern the motives behind brute facts. From a practical point of view, these efforts are not amiss in a world where "creative" financial transactions could bring down markets and nations.[1] They are going to become ever more necessary as time goes on, and they will be expanded to include the monitoring of virtually all of our actions, day in and day out.

Horrible as it may sound, this future is coming upon us more quickly than we are wont to believe. Make no mistake: when this future comes to pass, we—we who could see it, who knew it—we will be held responsible for it. The bloody garments of martyrs to come will be laid at our feet. The souls herded into hell by the prince of this world will be held to our account. History will damn us and the great cloud of witnesses in heaven will disown us.

Yet all is not doom and gloom. Many Christians have allowed themselves to be ruined with a suicidal theology that surrenders this world—God's world—to the devil and resigns itself to defeat as long as God does not intervene with supernatural events in the heavens. Such as these say there is no hope for the future. We can only expect greater and greater darkness and our only hope is to be whisked out of it. From such as these,

---

1 Be sure that this monitoring has to do with national security, not just drug trafficking.

we must walk away. They are the damned. They are the unfaithful stewards, who hid their light under a bushel, who buried their money in the ground. But who will be faithful with the Word of Truth, which can *well* light our way even in this darkness, and which is the weapon by which we shall conquer?

Instead of imagining a world in which the kingdom of hell is established on earth, consider the other possibility—a world in which God's kingdom is established in a greater way, where the truth is held in high esteem, and where righteousness grows greater from one generation to the next. Imagine a world where darkness has been deeply destroyed. Imagine a world overflowing with peace and freedom, and godly prosperity without sorrow.

Such a world is not beyond us. It is not too ethereal to behold. The Bible plainly lights the way to it. We won't get there by following polite reformers though. It's going to take a political revolution that challenges to the very core what people think and believe about government. With revolution, godly government is within our reach, if we want it. Without revolution, it is impossible. Polite reform just won't work.

Clearly, this is a sobering proposition, and one that should not be adopted lightly. Neither should it be *rejected* lightly, though. Revolution is a dangerous affair, and potentially deadly. Yet the future we face without it is *intolerable.* There are, after all, things worse than death. Millions upon millions of souls for untolled generations to come hang in the balance. They are not lost and without hope yet . . . not yet.

It is my purpose in this book to show that a godly revolution is both necessary and sufficient to solve the problems we face and create a livable future for godly men and women. Likewise it is my purpose to outline how that revolution can be initiated.

The biggest enemy we face in coming to this understanding is ourselves. Firstly, there is our own shallow mindedness. Simply put, we have no concrete vision of a better world. Like some foolish animal, we keep plodding along in the same old ruts because we know them so well. We've worn them so deep that we can't see out of them. We're content to send a few dollars to this or that cause, or support a stirring preacher. We're content to go to the polls and vote for the best candidate at election time, etc. Then we think we've done our duty. A few of us may take up this or that cause and fight hard. Yet in the end, we realize that we're likely to be no more successful than a child on the sea shore trying to stop the rising tide by bailing out the ocean with a bucket. Our strength for the battle wanes . . . yet we cannot get beyond the ruts others have worn.

In particular, we cannot see beyond individual issues, and so we are like an army with no common purpose. One man says abortion is the most important issue and fights there. Another says sound money is the most important, and puts his efforts into monetary reform. Another attacks the tyranny of the Revenue Service or corruption in government. Another attacks pornography. Still another attacks poverty. Our vision of a better society is fragmented and rootless though. We realize that even if we obtained a complete, devastating victory in one of these areas, whatever it might be, while the others were left alone, things would still be far from okay. Yet we don't really have any idea of what "okay" would be. Without an ideal, without a vision, we will settle for "barely tolerable" every time. We are too blind to know anything better. Like someone who has grown up in grinding poverty all his life, we don't know what it would be like to live in a house that provides real shelter from the rain, much less to cook on a gas stove, have running water, or use a machine to wash clothes. So we settle for a few crumbs and some soggy cardboard to put on the walls.

In my book *True Christian Government*, I attempted to remedy this shallow mindedness. Certainly, if we have no solid vision for what a godly society even is, we can never get there. In that book, I laid out the Bible's simple plan for human government. We looked at the scriptural justification for it, the rationale behind it, and the specific laws that a Christian community would have.[2] This is a picture of what should be. It is a country of unparalleled freedom, where God's will and godly people can prosper and grow in godliness. Neither is it something that must be established by a supernatural event. There is nothing about it that is impossible to implement, should a people wish to implement it.

Yet a clear vision for a better world is not enough. The truth is we have become comfortable and soft. We have the governments we have largely by consent. They buy the undying loyalties of their citizens with legislative favors and bribes. They cajole people into going along with all kinds of sins for the sake of personal gain, private peace and looking good before men. Christians are besotted by preachers who have bought into this agenda, and have learned to use the scriptures to legitimize and justify the creations of their own hands—specifically, the governments we have created—rather than to learn how to please God.

So, to a vision of a better world, we must add a certain moral zeal to lay aside what the multitude of men have to say, to scorn their favor, and to live as God has called us to, naming good and evil as God names it. There is a price to be paid to do this.

First we must understand that evil men will never love the truth or adopt it of their own accord. It doesn't matter how polite we are about it. Evil understands only force. It will yield only to force. Ignore this fact, and you cannot but become the stooge of evil men. Whoever lays aside truth for manners loses everything in the end. Evil men are not some theoretical possibility who only live at other times in history or in some other country. They are among us everywhere. They smile at us and bless us and breathe peace and prosperity, but they are as whitewashed tombs. All they really want you to do in the end is treat them with respect . . . and set their lie up as co-equal with the truth.

Yet we are polite because we do not properly weigh the truth. We fail to understand that in being polite, we are allowing truth to be overcome by brute force. In so doing, we are taking sides with the sons of darkness and not the sons of light. Yahweh

---

2 These laws are summarized in *Appendix A* of this book as well.

God will find out who our true gods are in this confrontation between force and truth, though. Do we value our traditions of representative government more than His Word? Shall we abide the truth being trampled under foot in the next election for the sake of upholding those traditions? If so, we'd better start figuring out how those traditions will save us.

To seriously consider revolution as a possible means to a godly society, we cannot be polite. Revolution is a total confrontation, a confrontation that involves questions too deep and too serious for mere politics to resolve. It involves change that goes beyond the legislature, the courts and the government. *It involves breaking the law.* Yet it is much more than a bloody rebellion or a *coup d'etat* that throws one person or group out of control of a government and installs another. Revolution is moral—it is all about morals—at heart it is a conflict of irreconcilable moral systems. It is a matter of essential, life and death faith, born out of an intelligent, informed commitment.

Understand, of course, that I am asking you to join me in this revolution. This book is not titled The *Christian Revolution*, or some such thing. It is titled *The Christian Revolutionary*. By that I mean *you*. In the end the revolutionary is a speaker of truth, and the truth is a great divider. Like Elijah over 2500 years ago, the time has come to say "Choose you this day whom you will serve. If Baal is God, serve him. If Yahweh is God, then serve him." You cannot serve God and mammon. You cannot continue to be holden to the traditions of men and yet be found complete in the sight of God. So it is my hope that by reading this book you, too, will come to believe that revolution is necessary and viable, and that a godly society and a better world are within reach, if we will but make the effort to reach. I hope you will realize that to reach is not beyond you. Finally, it is also my hope that you will be willing to pay the price necessary to become such a revolutionary. For that price I offer you a hope and a future.

*

CHAPTER 2

Revolution, Law and Morals

Revolution is not a bunch of desperate men with AK-47's in the jungles of Central America trying to overthrow the government. It is not an armed rebellion. It is not a *coup d'etat*, or plotting the violent overthrow of some government. It can *lead* to all of those things, but that is not what it *is*. At bottom, revolution is a conflict between moral systems, one well established, the other not.

The focal point of revolutionary controversy is law. That's because law, by its very nature, is a fundamental *expression* of right and wrong, of good and evil. Thus, the morality of any nation is expressed in its laws. This cannot be otherwise, for to forbid some action with a law is to assert that such an action is somehow wrong or bad. Otherwise, why forbid it? Why punish it? Likewise, something that is not forbidden is not wrong.

More deeply, *law is a teacher of morals*. Simply put, the law tells men what is right and wrong. Men learn to obey the law if only for practical reasons, and they learn to rationalize their obedience in terms of basic morality.

So revolution—as a moral controversy—must boil down to law. Different morals require different laws for their expression. Morals become established through law. Different laws teach different morals. Thus a revolution that did not change the law could not be said to have truly changed the ruling morality, and

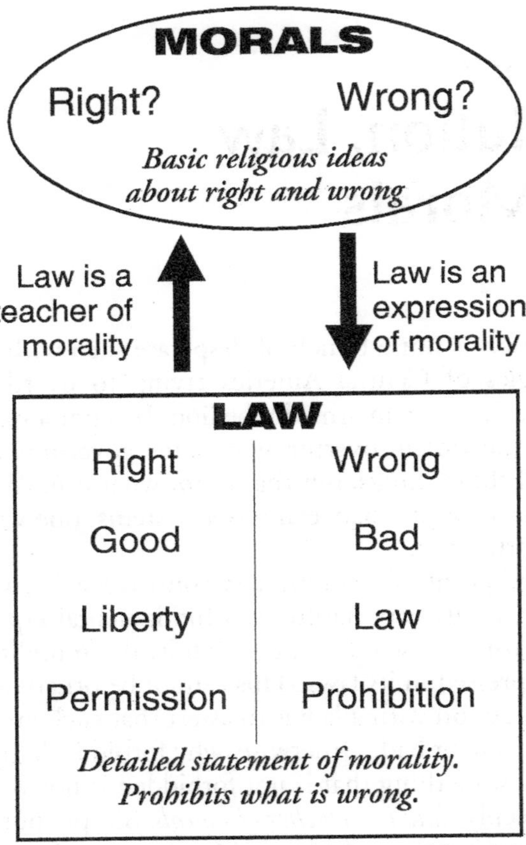

it could not survive because the old law would continue to teach people to accept the old morality.

In modern times, revolutions have tended to advance their ideas under the banner of liberty or rights, rather than in terms of law. Certainly the idea of liberties and rights is more stirring than "law". However, liberty is intimately associated with law. Morally speaking, what is not forbidden is permitted. One has a right to do what is not wrong. To the extent that any moral system is established, its prohibitions will be respected and its liberties will be explored. Law will establish the prohibitions and open up the liberties. So liberty, too, is essentially a matter of morals and law.

In revolutionary times, people come to question the law and its foundations. It ceases to be the silent purveyor of morals. Its basic *rightness* is no longer taken for granted. Laws are said to be unjust and therefore invalid, and laws that are not valid need not be obeyed. New principles of law are held forward to both negate the old and establish the new.

We can see this principle at work in all the great revolutions of the past. The communists abolished the entire legal system of old Russia in favor of no laws and no legal system (at first) because even *nothing* was better than a legal system that was a formulation of bourgeois oppression. The French to this day celebrate the liberation of the king's prison on Bastille Day, the liberation of men held by the king's law being symbolic of the fall of the king's law. The American colonists' slogan "no taxation without representation" points up their antipathy toward "arbitrary" tax laws, and by implication, "arbitrary" laws in general. Cromwell had England's king and lawgiver executed for breaking the law. Luther burned the canon law books of the Catholic Church.

In each case, revolution was essentially a contest about law, the morality of the law, and the principle upon which a just legal system could be founded.

At the same time, there are contests going on over law all the time, and they can hardly be said to be indicative of a budding revolution. Congresses and parliaments the world around are continually lobbied to pass or repeal various laws. Sometimes the debate is hot, and may last for years. Likewise, questions of law are continually being taken up by courts with no apparent destabilizing effects. Such questions are often serious moral questions, but they do not lead to revolution and the dissolution of a government. Somehow, revolution is something more than a mere legal or moral *question*.

Where revolution differs is that it involves *fundamental principles* that are generally not resolvable within the system.

The moral conflict becomes a revolution because it is of fundamental importance, yet the system does not or cannot resolve it. From a practical perspective, the system suffers from some fatal flaw that prevents a resolution. Generally speaking, this fatal flaw is of a philosophical or theological nature such that resolution cannot be had without undermining the whole foundation of the law of the old regime.

Thus, the Catholic Church could not accept Luther's idea about justification by faith because it had built up a tradition over the past five hundred years concerning purgatory and penance. Since the turn of the millennium, purgatory had gained an official status as a place where Christians paid for sins they had committed after baptism, while Christ's atonement had been reduced to a mere atonement for an abstraction called original sin, not actual sins committed by real persons. This theological idea formed the foundation for the legal system of the Catholic Church as well as many of its institutions. Justification by faith did away with the idea that a Christian must pay for all his sins by being tortured in some netherworld. That was the hold which the Catholic Church had on people though. Justification by faith undercut the entire system of penance and indulgences, and denied the power of the Pope to lock a man out of heaven at a word. Practically speaking, the Pope's tremendous temporal power had come to rest on his power to open or close heaven. Justification by faith undermined it all. The Catholic Church could not change itself to conform to this idea without major dislocation, and truly, without calling all their actions of the past five hundred years into question and being driven to establish a whole new theory of its political authority. What might be called the first modern revolution ensued.

The French, English and American revolutions brought down the idea of the divine right of kings, which was being asserted ever more persistently after the reformation had reduced the Pope's stature (even in catholic countries). A major theme driving these revolutions was the relationship of the king to the law. The king asserted that he was a divinely appointed lawgiver and, as such, above the law. His word was law *because* he was the divinely appointed lawgiver. Revolutionary thinkers claimed the king was—like other men—under the law, subject to it, and accountable to it. Looking to scripture or within themselves, the revolutionaries found new principles to give the law legitimacy. These new principles depended upon the vote of representatives of the people, who could weigh proposed laws, and insure that they were just and wise. Such representatives were both subject to the law and responsible to the people, who could recall them. Once again, these new principles were fundamentally incompatible with the old. If the law was king, then the king was an ordinary man. His word could be wrong and unjust according to a higher law, so the very principle of the kingdom was at stake. Every law the kings of old had ever made, every law that every future king might make would be continually subject to questioning and rejection on the basis that it violated some higher law. Only if the king was the highest law could his laws be inviolate. The idea of a law higher than the king properly overthrew the very principle of the kingdom, just as Luther's "*sola scriptura*" overthrew the principle of the papal church.

The communist revolutions of the twentieth century likewise asserted the existence of a higher law to challenge representative government. A philosophical principle of social justice and social and economic equality was posited to be the highest law. This principle rendered unjust the law created by a king, a tsar, or a legislature, if that law did not prove faithful to the principle. In particular, laws which acted in the interest of nobility, of capitalists, of the bourgeoisie at the expense of the proletariat underclass were seen as fundamentally unjust. This principle has threatened the representative system of government throughout most of the 20th century, and still does threaten it deeply, even if most people are not aware of that. Although communism, *per se*, seems to be receding at present, the concept of a higher ideal of social justice continues to advance. To some extent, representative governments have espoused the concept of social justice and implemented the program of the communists. Yet communism is fundamentally an elitist philosophy that leads to an ideological oligarchy. Modern governments trying to accommodate the principle of social justice have thus moved unilaterally toward bureaucratic rule, and away from accountability to the people and their votes. That accountability is maintained for the present, but it cannot ultimately survive the accession of social justice—or any other philosophical principle—to the place of the highest law. If it is unjust for the majority to pass a law that hurts a minority (according to whatever philosophical principle is in vogue) then the system of government that propagates an unjust majority rule is itself unjust and must ultimately be done away with. At present there are various elite groups seeking center stage with their versions of social justice. These range from economic egalitarianism to environmentalism to non-proliferation to free trade and so on. All march under the banner of social justice, and as far as representative government is concerned, it matters little which one gains control in the end.

In every case, revolution involves a contest of legal principles that cannot be resolved within the system of the old regime, and which fundamentally challenge the legal principles which legitimize the laws of the old regime. Thus revolutions are both moral crusades and unlawful at the same time—moral crusades to reform the immoral old system, and unlawful by the standards of the old system.

Since revolution can be both moral and unlawful at the same time, some kind of violence is a normal product of revolution. Either the revolutionaries will confront a corrupt and immoral system by refusing to obey its immoral laws and reaping the consequences, or the rulers of the old system will recognize the threat and outlaw the revolution. One way or another, the revolutionaries become outlaws according to the old laws. Yet the controversy is essentially legal and moral. In the end, the revolutionary is not a gun-toting mad man, but a true believer in a higher moral principle.

Very well, with this much in mind, it is now time to look at the basic moral principles which undergird the modern state, and the moral principle of the Bible. *We cannot begin to under-*

stand how Christian reform can possibly work in this age unless these moral principles are clear in our minds. In particular, they are fundamentally incompatible and incapable of reconciliation, so reform must inevitably take revolutionary overtones or it will fail.

CHAPTER 3

The Moral Principles of the Bible

It is commonplace in the present age to assert that the scripture has little to say about the *form* of government we choose to adopt. Were this not so often repeated, it would be hard to believe, in as much as government is all about law, what the laws will be and why . . . why we should have the laws we do and why we should obey them. Every form of government engenders some theory of law that makes law law. Since law is a moral determination of right and wrong, it hardly seems probable that the Bible has nothing to say about it. After all, scripture is all about right and wrong. Therefore we might say it is all about law and government. To understand it, though, we have to start with basics that have been clouded over for a long time.

The scriptures plainly teach, from beginning to end, that God is the one who determines right and wrong. His judgments concerning what is right and wrong, what is good and evil, are alone true. Those judgments are also final, in as much as God is the final judge of the world, who alone has the power to cast into hell, or to open heaven.

In the beginning, God told Adam that he could not eat of the tree of the knowledge of good and evil. This was the one and only command that Adam had. When Adam and Eve broke that command, they sinned and incurred the punishment of God. Yet that sin was not something abstract that we cannot understand, some mystical "original sin" in which men ate from a mystical tree in a mythical paradise. The tree could have been any tree. Clearly its fruit was not poison. It became the tree of the knowledge of good and evil *by virtue of God's command.* As the creator, and as the one who determines right and wrong, God had the right to say one tree is off limits. By virtue of His command it became the tree of the knowledge of good and evil. Man could obey God, and come to a godly understanding of good and evil, or he could disobey. By disobeying, he would put away God's determination of good and evil, and judge for himself that what God said to be evil was actually good. By eating of the tree, he would claim the ability to determine good and evil for himself.

Ever since Adam and Eve ate from the tree, man's problem has been his unwillingness to accept God's determination of good and evil, right and wrong. Instead man has claimed the right to make such determinations for himself. The scriptures, however, never yield such a prerogative to man. Rather, the Bible is constant in maintaining that God alone can make such determinations.

God's law *defines* what is right and wrong. It is the very standard of what is good and what is evil, the scriptural statement of what is moral and immoral:

> "by the law is the knowledge of sin."—*Romans 3:20*

> "Whosoever committeth sin transgresseth also the law: for sin is the transgression of the law."—*I John 3:4*

Men today try to reason God's commandments away and say that they were meant for thousands of years ago, and they are just nice "moral precepts" today, or they say that love does away with the law, and so on and so forth. They fail to realize that if there is no law, there is no sin

> "where no law is, there is no transgression"—*Romans 4:15*

Without the definition of sin, how can there be sin? Yet if there is no sin, men are sinless and have no need of a savior. Thus, such claims about God's law make Christ unnecessary and his sacrifice of no purpose, calling God a liar:

> "If we say that we have not sinned, we make him a liar, and his word is not in us."—*1 John 1:10*

Obedience to God's commandments is stressed again and again in the scriptures, from Genesis to Revelation. The Old Testament is so full of such references there is not room to quote them. Jesus himself affirmed that obedience is essential:

> "Not everyone that saith unto me 'Lord, Lord,' shall enter into the kingdom of heaven, but *he that doeth the will of my Father* which is in heaven . . . . Therefore whosoever heareth these sayings of mine, *and doeth them,* I will liken him unto a wise man, which built his house upon a rock."—*Matthew 7:21,24*

> "If thou wilt enter into life, *keep the commandments.*"—*Matthew 19:17*

> "If ye love me, *keep my commandments.*"—*John 14:15*

> "He that hath my commandments, and *keepeth them,* he it is that loveth me."—*John 14:21*

> "He that loveth me not *keepeth* not my sayings."—*John 14:24*

> "If ye *keep my commandments,* ye shall abide in my love; even as I have kept my Father's commandments, and abide in his love."—*John 15:10*

> "Blessed are they that hear the word of God and keep it."—*Luke 11:28*

If we believe that Jesus was God incarnate, then "my commandments" does not mean just the sermon on the mount, or the words printed in red. It means all of God's commands.

Those that keep, or *do* what God says are blessed. They—and they alone—are the ones who love God. It is they who have eternal life. Jesus taught this, and the apostles affirmed it:

> "Circumcision is nothing, and uncircumcision is nothing, *but the keeping of the commandments of God.*"—*1 Corinthians 7:19*

Circumcision of the heart is what counts. John equates knowing and loving God with keeping his commands:

> "And hereby we do know that we know him, *if we keep his commandments.* He that saith, 'I know him,' and keepeth not his commandments, is a liar, and the truth is not in him."—*1 John 2:3,4*

> "And whatsoever we ask, we receive of him, *because we keep his commandments,* and do those things that are pleasing in his sight."—*1 John 3:22*

> "By this we know that we love the children of God, when we love God, and *keep his commandments.* For this is the love of God, that we *keep his commandments*: and his commandments are not grievous."—*1 John 5:2,3*

By implication, if His commandments are grievous and we keep them grudgingly, it's evidence that we're not His.

> "And *this is love, that we walk after his commandments.* This is the commandment, that, as ye have heard from the beginning, ye should walk in it."—*2 John 6*

And those who keep the commandments are the children of God who inherit eternal life:

> "And the dragon was wroth with the woman, and went to make war with the remnant of her seed, *which keep the commandments of God,* and have the testimony of Jesus Christ."—*Revelation 12:17*

> "Here is the patience of the saints: here are they that *keep the commandments* of God, and the faith of Jesus."—*Revelation 14:12*

> "Blessed are they that *do his commands,* that they may have right to the tree of life, and may enter in through the gates into the city."—*Revelation 22:14*

There is no other standard. There is no other measure of right and wrong, but God's determinations. Scripturally speaking, therefore, the moral principle—the principle that makes law legitimate—is God's word.

BIBLICAL LIBERTY

The scriptures also make it very plain that man has no authority to change God's law. He may not add to it. He may not take away from it. This is a fundamental principle of the law:

> "Ye shall not add unto the word which I command you, neither shall ye diminish ought from it, that ye may keep the commandments of the LORD your God which I command you."—*Deuteronomy 4:2*

> "What thing soever I command you, observe to do it: thou shall not add thereto, nor diminish from it."—*Deuteronomy 12:32*

It stands as basic wisdom:

> "Every word of God is pure: he is a shield unto them that put their trust in him. Add thou not unto his words, lest he reprove thee, and thou be found a liar."—*Proverbs 30:5,6*

is affirmed by Christ:

> "Till heaven and earth pass, one jot or one tittle shall in no wise pass from the law, till all be fulfilled. Whosoever therefore shall break one of these least commandments, and shall teach men so, he shall be called the least in the kingdom of heaven."—*Matthew 5:18,19*

affirmed by the apostles:

> "Christ hath redeemed us from the curse of the law, being made a curse for us: for it is written, Cursed is every one that hangeth on a tree: That the blessing of Abraham might come on the Gentiles through Jesus Christ: that we might receive the promise of the Spirit through faith. Brethren, I speak after the manner of men; *Though it be but a man's covenant, yet if it be confirmed, no man disannulleth, or addeth thereto.*"--*Galatians 3:13-15*

and it stands until the end of time:

> "For I testify unto every man that heareth the words of the prophecy of this book, If any man shall add unto these things, God shall add unto him the plagues that are written in this book; and if any man shall take away from the words of the book of this prophecy, God shall take away his part out of the book of life . . . ."—*Revelation 22:18,19*

To change God's word and commandments is to commit the same sin Adam and Eve did *all over again*. It is to claim a better knowledge of good and evil than God.

The reason for such a prohibition is stated clearly in Deuteronomy 4:2, "that ye may keep the commandments of the LORD." To change God's laws and confuse them keeps men from keeping them. Since God's law is a tutor to lead men to Christ (Galatians 3:24) it stands to reason that if His law is changed, it will lead to something other than Christ. This is exactly what Jesus taught:

> "In vain do they worship me, teaching for doctrines the commandments of men, for laying aside the commandment of God, ye hold the tradition of men . . . . Full well *ye reject the commandment of God, that ye may keep your own tradition.* For Moses said, Honor thy father and thy mother; and, whoso curseth father or mother, let him die the death. But ye say, If a man shall say to his father or mother, 'It is Corban, that is to say, a gift, by whatsoever thou mightest be profited by me,' he shall be free. And ye suffer him no more to do ought for his father or his mother, *making the word of God of none effect through your tradition."—Mark 7:7-13*

> "This people draweth nigh unto me with their mouth, and honoureth me with their lips; but their heart is far from me. But *in vain they do worship me, teaching for doctrines the commandments of men."—Matthew 15:8,9*

The word of God is made of no effect when we reason it away and change it with our traditions.

In our sophisticated modern age we reason away scriptures like Deuteronomy 4:2 and divide law into divine law and secular laws. Then we say that secular laws have nothing to do with divine law, and by making a secular law we are not changing the divine law. We call a breach of the secular law "crime" and a breach of the divine law "sin", and say the two are different matters. The truth, of course, is that *all* law is a teacher or tutor. It is only a question of *what* it is teaching men to do, and what it is teaching them to believe to be right and wrong. Any law that does not agree with scripture is, at the very least, teaching men a human standard for right and wrong. Indeed, if God forbids something and man permits it, man is saying that God is wrong. Or if God permits something and man forbids it, then man is claiming a knowledge of good and evil that exceeds God's. Isn't this exactly what Jesus condemned in his teaching about corban? So the claim that we are not adding to or taking away from what is written by making "secular" law is patently false. Likewise, if we decide that God's remedy for some particular sin is incorrect, and prescribe a different remedy, are we not again setting ourselves up as God's judges and changing His laws?

The moral principle of the Bible is thus exactly what God says in the Bible, no more and no less, *because He is God.* Man is to obey without changing the law. This moral principle works itself out in law with the assertion that *a law is only legitimate if it is God's law.* Those laws are spelled out in the Bible.[1] To add to or take away from or otherwise change what is written is itself an illegal act, and sin. Any laws which do that are illegitimate.

This prohibition against changing God's law is thus the fundamental law of liberty in the Bible. What God has not forbidden, *man is free to explore.* What God has not delegated to man to punish is a private matter between God and the individual.

Needless to say, if we keep our morality private it can remain polite, but if we apply it to the legal sphere it becomes a pretty strong statement, both in terms of law and liberty. Yet this strong statement is necessary in order for God's judgments about right and wrong to stand at all. Were men allowed to sit in judgement on God's laws, God would not be God. Man could define away his sin, and do away with any need for a savior, or for God. That would appear to be exactly what modern men have done. But does that mean we should take this moral principle of scripture out of the private sphere and press it in the public arena of law? Before we answer that question, let us examine the two other moral systems at work in the world today.

1 I have examined these laws as pertain to a community government in detail in my book *True Christian Government.*

CHAPTER 4

The Moral Principles of Representative Government

In recent times there has been a controversy between Christians and secularists as to whether modern constitutional republics were conceived as Christian nations or not. The Christians say they were, and point to the personal faith of founders and the population at large. Secularists, on the other hand, point to the fact that others of the founders were innovators in religion and that the founding documents of such nations make little mention of God and none of Jesus Christ.

At least some modern republics clearly were conceived by Christian men with the specific understanding that a Christian morality would inform the system, even though that morality was not explicitly incorporated into that system. It would also appear that, at least in nations with a strong protestant heritage, the morality of the people did inform the system. At the same time, the *system* of government of the modern republics was not itself dependent on Christianity. Mechanically it could work just as well under Islam, or in an atheistic society.

This whole controversy has the really important question backwards though. ***It is not how the pre-existing morality of a people shapes the system that is so important in the long run, but how the machinery of the system shapes the morality of the people.*** In as much as the system is *designed to make laws,* it is designed to issue pronouncements of morality, and therefore to teach morality. That is simply its nature. Therefore the system itself has a moral principle implicit in it, which will shape the morality of those subject to it.

Because law is a teacher of morality, no system of government can be truly morally neutral. Every system necessarily establishes certain principles as the moral absolutes by which everything else will be judged. Simply put, every time a question about the legitimacy of any law arises, it is the principles used to decide that question which are the final moral principles of the nation.

In a democratic republic, this final moral principle is the vote. Constitutions delineate procedures for lawmaking. Elected legislatures propose bills and vote on them. Elected presidents, governors or prime ministers sign bills into law, or veto them, and legislatures can generally override a veto by approving a bill with a super-majority. Although constitutions generally place limits on the lawmaking power, these limits are *not* absolute. The same constitutions provide procedures whereby they can be amended or even dissolved entirely. Once again, such procedures depend on the vote—perhaps the votes of different people, in different numbers, but the vote none the less. Though there be ever so many procedures and levels of representation in between, everything ultimately distills down to the vote.

In principle, then, there is no limit to what might be made lawful or unlawful in a constitutional republic, only provided it has sufficient popular support. There is nothing to stop the passage of a constitutional amendment that demands everyone with blue eyes be put to death. Any abominable or bizarre law one might imagine could, in principle, be put into effect. The system for creating laws provides no absolute limits in the sense of a religious morality, so long as the proper procedure is followed. Whatever limits exist in actual practice do not come from the machinery of the system, but from the voters themselves. The law is limited only by what men can conceive and only by what voters will tolerate. If there are any limits at all, they have to come from beyond the system.

As far as the system itself is concerned, *law can only be illegitimate in so far as it has not gone through the proper procedures to become law.* A bill that was made law without the proper authorization by the legislature would be an example of an illegitimate law. An ordinary law which violated a constitutional limit would be an illegitimate law. To become legitimate, it would have to be passed as an amendment. Likewise, rules promulgated by a bureaucracy that went beyond its delegated authority would be illegitimate. Such issues are generally up to the courts to decide. It is the courts which either uphold the laws and command their provisions to be met out, or nullify them as illegitimate.

Within the context of the system, no legitimate law can ever be immoral. It can be immoral in the sense of being illegitimate, e.g., unconstitutional, etc., but not otherwise. It can only be called "immoral" from a position external to the system. However, "external to the system" ultimately means *foreign* to the system. To call a law that has been duly established "immoral" is to set oneself up in judgement of the *system.* Thus, one cannot argue in a state established court that a law should be annulled because it is *immoral,* unscriptural, etc. One can argue for annullment on the basis of *unconstitutionality,* or because the law was improperly enacted according to the procedures specified in the constitution or because it conflicts with another duly established law. If one deems a law to be immoral, the only lawful recourse is to work to get enough popular support to overturn the law through legislative channels . . . in other words, use the founding principle of the republic—the vote—to change the law. As such, there can be no appeal to a higher law outside the system. The vote is the final moral principle of a democratic republic. The people and their will is the highest authority. *Vox populi, vox dei* . . . the voice of the people is the voice of God. No particular moral, as expressed in law, can be valid without popular approval, as detailed in the constitution. No moral as expressed in properly ratified law can be invalid within the context of the system.

Thus, the constitutional republic cannot be viewed as a morally neutral form of government. Rather, it is its own self-consistent moral system that will subvert and overcome any other moral system through politics and the constitution. This moral system is not at all like traditional moral systems which posit absolute truths about specific human actions. It does not, for example, insist that murder or adultery are wrong in any absolute sense. They are wrong if the voters want them to be wrong in the contexts that the voters want them to be wrong, and they are not wrong if the voters don't want them to be wrong. Immorality consists (1) of laws being imposed upon people without their consent, and (2) of the breaking of legitimate laws, whatever they may be at the moment.

If a representative system of government forms a moral system, then its constitution is essentially the holy writ. It should not therefore be surprising that similarities abound between a constitutional polity and the church. Thus, for example, citizens are typically divided over their constitutions. There are "catholics" who believe the constitution can only be properly understood within the context of the traditions of the republic and the pronouncements of the court. There are protestants who desire to return to the original intent of the founders. Battles between the two factions can take on the dimensions of religious wars and so forth.[1]

How Traditional Morals are Subverted

Historically, the subversion of traditional morality by representative government is accomplished as legislatures, presidents and judges attempt to enlarge their jurisdiction. In so doing, they test hypothetical limits on their legislative power. The only limits that will consistently withstand such testing are

1 Sanford Levinson has explored the dimensions of this analogy with a traditional religious system in his poignant book, *Constitutional Faith* (Princeton University Press, 1988)

those that are set in stone, which to do away with would be to do away with the republic itself. Thus the law will expand to fill the limits allowed for it by what is written. People naturally resist that expansion all along, because every attempt at expansion is innovative. It offends someone's traditional sense of what is right and wrong. However, every innovation written into the law becomes a teacher of a new morality. So in time, people are trained to accept the innovation, and indeed, after some time, to go back would involve renewed moral innovation because the new morals have been completely ingrained into the subconscious of the people. The machinery of most republics actually seems to *favor* morally subversive politics. New laws typically require only a simple majority. Yet irresponsible lawmakers must be removed from office by a super-majority, and even then, their bad laws are not off the books! Thus it is much easier to create new laws—new morals—than it is to punish innovative or subversive lawmakers.

PERSONAL MORALITY

The law as a teacher of morality teaches not only specific morals, "do not do this or that", but as it grows and explores its limits it also begins to teach the moral *principles* which underlie the moral specifics—moral principles that apply not just at the civic level, but personally. So the system takes on moral overtones that overshadow any of the earlier morality which may have existed when the system was established.

The modern representative state is the incubator in which the modern philosophy that "there are no absolutes" grew strong. Indeed, there *are* no absolutes in a constitutional republic. The entire government is man's creation and it institutionalizes the idea that man's word is law. That is the one absolute that everything must bow down to. Man's word is law *because* it is man's word. The absolutes of God's word are the ultimate tyranny and the ultimate immorality because men never consented to them or voted on them. Thus, any such absolutes must be rejected. They must be no more. They must be done away with.

So the philosophy of "there are no absolutes" is merely a personal application of the great principle of representative government. The voice of the people is free to control anything, to outlaw or permit anything. What that social voice chooses to leave a private matter is—in mirror image of the civil government—entirely up to the individual to decide based on his personal will. To that extent he can believe what he wishes and live as he sees fit.

THE PRINCIPLE OF LIBERTY

In a representative state, the only absolute liberty is that no one has to submit to a law that has not been properly legitimized by the machinery of government.[2] The constitutions of various governments may enshrine various rights and liberties, however these liberties are not absolute. They are guaranteed only in so far as they cannot be changed, dismantled or reasoned away. Typically, liberties enshrined in a constitution become fixated in the popular mind as basic values of the society, so they do have some protection—the voice of the people will not quickly tolerate their abolition.

None the less, the principles of liberty in a constitutional republic are extremely limited. Liberty is not open ended, but rather, it consists of a closed set of statements. Anything else is fair game for easy legislative regulation, as needed, to effect the popular will. Even so, legislation is generally proposed only when someone sees a need for it. Thus, a representative government may be perceived as a relatively free government when first established. It may remain relatively free for a long time too. Though every area of life is potentially open to regulation, legislatures generally don't take some perverse pleasure in enslaving the people they represent. They only do it when they deem it necessary for the furtherance of some higher purpose,

---

2 Of course, there is always the question of what "properly legitimized" really means. That is always decided by those in power, who naturally favor their own agendas and discard the original intent of dead founders.

especially for the preservation of the republic. However, necessity is always the gateway to slavery and tyranny. Freedom always takes a back seat to presumed necessity.

Here we already begin to see the fundamental incompatibility between the moral principle of scripture and the moral principle of representative government. Either God's word is law *because* it is God's word, or man's word is law *because* it is man's word. Both logically deny one another. Before we explore the full implications of this fact, though, there is one more moral principle to consider.

CHAPTER 5

The Moral Principles of the Ideological Elite

From the very beginning, representative government has involved strong undercurrents of elitism. Indeed, we might say that the idea of a constitutional republic would never have had a chance except there were some mixture of elitism involved in its creation from the beginning. No educated person really believes that an illiterate woodsman who's never been more than five miles from where he was born would know what is good for society at large. That is why early thinkers and founders of the modern republics universally rejected pure democracy in favor of a representative republic which combined ideas ranging from Plato's *Republic* to the election of King Saul found in 1 Samuel 10:24. Good but simple people may not be able to resolve difficult issues of government, but they could recognize a good and intelligent man and elect him to represent them.

In the late twentieth century, the distinction between democracy and republic has been blurred in the dumbing down process of public education. At the same time, the elitism inherent in a republic has actually become more pronounced. Indeed, one could foresee a point in the not too distance future in which that elitism could openly eclipse democratic institutions altogether.

One must be realistic about the elitism inherent in a republic. It is one thing to read Rousseau describing democracy as a government for the gods and saying that some elected aristocracy (e.g. republic) is the best government for men. We have been taught to agree with such statements. At the same time, a more blunt statement of the same thing might prove offensive:

> "The individuals see the good they reject, the public wills the good it does not see. All stand equally in need of guidance. The former must be compelled to bring their wills into conformity with their reason; the latter must be taught to know what it wills."[1]

To say that the unwashed masses—the other guy—needs guidance, compulsion and enlightenment is one thing. Some of us do that much every day. To admit that *I* need it is something else. We may be tempted to reject Rousseau as some pedantic philosopher. Yet such sentiments were not uncommon in the 18th century. For example, George Washington, often called the father of the United States, said about the same thing:

> "Experience has taught us that men will not adopt and carry into execution measures the best calculated for their own good, without the intervention of a coercive power."[2]

More seriously, these ideas are woven into the constitutions of modern republics and have come to permeate the political realities of nations.

A significant change has taken place between then and now, though. When governments are formed, the ideals of the revolutionaries are the ideals enshrined in national constitutions, the ideals that animated the movements for independence, etc. As such, the elite's ideals are not initially subversive of the new government itself. How could they be if they gave birth to it? Yet, as time goes on, the pull of various ideals can change, and people who hold different ideals dear can rise to power. To the extent that such idealists are willing to submit their ideals to the higher ideal of representative government, those ideals need not be a threat to the system. However, if that ideal is elevated to

---

1 Rousseau, *The Social Contract and Discourses*, (J.M. Dent and Sons, London:1973) p. 213.
2 Letter to John Jay, August 1, 1786

the level of a moral principle, it comes into conflict with the moral principle of representative government, and threatens its very foundations.

This elevation of idealism to basic morality occurred as early as the French Revolution, in which the basic needs of poverty stricken people were enshrined in the ideals of the revolutionaries and became a motivating force that destroyed the revolutionary government, destroyed any prospect for a national constitution and drove the revolution into terror and anarchy. Atrocities were necessary for the sake of the suffering masses. The needs of the people became the measure of morality, and what was traditionally "crime" or "sin" was not seen as such if carried out to alleviate the peoples' suffering. These ideas were later formalized and carried to their logical conclusion by Marx.

Marxism and its later forms of Lenninist, Maoist and Gramscian communism are essentially an idealism that appeals to elitists and intellectuals. Although Marx had a lot to say about the working class, or proletariat, it was the elite who were attracted to his ideas. Wherever his ideas were put into practice, they have produced elitist governments which have often made the simple working class suffer greatly. And elitist intellectuals are still the vanguard of Marxism today.

Communism, however, remains the most logically consistent idealism in the world today. Making the ideal of economic equality the moral principle, the traditional Leninist-Marxist has no qualms about lying and cheating, destroying property, killing people who are in the way, overthrowing governments, and sending millions who do not share their moral principles to extermination camps. At bottom, their ideal is the determiner of right and wrong. Economic oppression is the Absolute Evil. Economic equality is the Absolute Good. Anything done to destroy oppression and foster equality is, by definition, good.

This idealism comes in conflict with representative government simply because representative government is founded on different morals. Of course, everyone should want the communist utopia where all is peace and plenty. However, so the reasoning goes, the bourgeois governments of the world keep the proletariat drugged with religion and games, and brainwash them with bourgeois public education, teaching them to be good little slaves. They're given a choice between two or three capitalist candidates to choose from in elections, etc. Thus, the larger part of humanity can hardly be expected to know what is good for them, and those that do cannot practically express it through the existing systems of government. Therefore, the dedicated communist cannot believe in representative government as a principle. As a form of government useful for advancing the communist ideal, he may make use of representative forms of government. Yet if that form of government begins to subvert communism instead of promote it, the communist, as an idealist committed to communism, will do away with that form of government rather than let the truth be subverted. The ideal is the absolute moral principle.

Of course, communism is by no means the only idealism that has vied for control in the past two centuries. It may be the most logically consistent, and the most implemented idealism, but it is hardly alone. To it we must add everything from the racialism of Nazi Germany to radical environmentalism to libertarianism and everything in between. Each of these "isms" make an idea the moral principle which determines right and wrong, just and unjust. Ultimately, they are at war with the moral principle behind representative government. Whether we're talking Adolf Hitler's destruction of representative government in Germany, tyrannical environmental regulations worked out in the obscure bowels of government agencies, or Ayn Rand's vision of the induced ruin of representative government in *Atlas Shrugged*, all of the idealists ultimately make their ideal the absolute by which all actions should be judged—the moral principle.

All idealists are also necessarily at war with traditional forms of morality, including Christian morality. Thus, Hitler did not flinch at murdering anyone who got in his way, be they Jews or Christians. Such were, in his moral system, not merely impediments to his progress, but people whose absence would materially benefit mankind. By the same token, environmentalists can join hands with Communist China and promote both forced abortion and forced sterilization because they reason that smaller populations and decreasing populations are good. Again, Ayn Rand had to create immoral characters and revel in immorality herself, rejecting traditional Christian moral responsibilities, in a world where self came first in all things.

Such actions are not inconsistent. When an idea is made the absolute by which good and evil are judged, it becomes a moral system unto itself, to which everything else must yield. Traditional as well as popular ideas of right and wrong must yield. Individuals must yield. Nations and peoples must yield.

Where many idealists are still inconsistent is that they still kiss the touchstone of democracy. They have not fully taken the step of going to war with the moral principle of the democratic republic. However, they increasingly work to subvert the democratic principle. In word, they still maintain that they favor representative government, yet they increasingly manipulate the public with propaganda and lies, and attempt to regulate the state outside the usual channels of accountability to the public (for example, through non-elected bureaucrats). To the extent that they can, they use money power to subvert the democratic process, buying politicians and the media. Others have become part of the media or have bought the organs of the media so they can push their ideas and shape public opinion in the tradition of Rousseau and Washington.

None the less, these attempts to manipulate and regulate the state must be understood as the first steps of various idealists to animate their ideals with a life of their own, quite independent of the representative state.

THE IDEAL BEHIND THE IDEALS

All of the idealists of the 20th century have legitimized their ideals on the grounds that they were working for the greatest good of mankind as a whole. Individuals, peoples, and nations may have to submit their short-sighted, selfish desires to that end, but such a demand is not essentially different from what men must already do in a democratic republic. When a candidate people don't like is elected, or a law they don't agree with is passed, they submit to that candidate or law to preserve the integrity of the republic.

Thus, the abstract idea of "the greatest good of mankind" for all generations would appear to be the principle by which ideals become accepted as legitimate. In a way, it has become the ideal behind all the ideas which are the banners of the modern age. At the same time, this "greatest good of mankind" is too vacuous—at least for the present—to be considered a moral principle. People argue that all kinds of things promote this good, but it has no real independent life of its own. Ideas are legitimized with greatest good arguments, but the process of legitimizing an idea is not scientific, rational or mechanical in any sense. Certainly it is nothing like how a law is legitimized in a democratic republic. Rather, these arguments become widely accepted through a process of no-holds-barred power politics. In any event, man is still just as much the measure of all things as he is in a republic.

In the end, the ideological elites' moral principles differ but little from that of representative government. The elite still make man's word law, just like representative government. Where they differ is their elitism. Not every man's word, not every man's vote should count equally because some are enlightened and others are not. The truly enlightened alone can make reasonable decisions. So, although the elite challenge the republic's morals, they don't succeed in going beyond them. They only establish an exclusionary principle to justify making themselves lords over others without their consent.

This is practically worked out in the republic in that laws don't just originate with the people. They often originate from various elites. The voice of the people in a republic rules not only by expressing positive desires in elections. It must also rule by expressing clearly *what it will not tolerate*, as is the situation when some ideologue decides the people need some new law and begins to work for it, or puts it in place by executive order, legislative fiat, or whatever.

This is a very important aspect of the development of law in a representative republic because often people will tolerate many things that they would not consciously decide they want. Much of the legal and moral development in a republic occurs in this manner.

However, just because that is the case doesn't mean the voice of the people has been somehow thwarted by the elite. Statements like Washington's and Rousseau's are more accurate than we might care to think. Men *do* often need to be shown what they want. And they certainly need a measure of coercion before any law or idea will even have a chance to work. So, for example, a crisis develops and people want out of the crisis, but they may not know how to get out of it. Ideas about how to get out of the crisis rarely rise up from the earth, so to speak. Rather, someone with a bright idea steps to center stage and people are attracted to him and his ideas. He is given power to put them into practice and make them into laws. Unless those who don't like his ideas can gain enough support to get rid of this new politician and his laws, they must submit to those ideas.

This is part of the normal political process in a republic. The fact that the republic can accommodate strong-minded people with ideals is part of its strength, and not a weakness. Unless such people could be accommodated, they would work to wreck the republic. They can work for their ideals and yet kiss the touchstone of democracy, while the people can still reject the worst of them and prevent them from poisoning the nation.

*

CHAPTER 6
Why Good Men Fail

That reform in the modern state always seems to fail is an unsettling observation which most traditional Christians are unwilling to face. Yet the record speaks for itself. Time after time, reformers have failed to carry their agenda and implement meaningful and lasting reform. When that happens, it is easy to blame powerful opponents, saying the reform movement is out-financed, out-lobbied and out-manned in the legislature. Certainly all of these obstacles serve as a platform for fund-raising efforts by reformers.

However, as these failures are repeated year after year, *ad nauseam*, it becomes imperative to ask why all efforts at reform fail, recognizing the well worn excuses as mere symptoms of a deeper problem. Why is it that the old guard of the old morality cannot maintain a steady line of defense, when every idealist and innovative special interest seems to get their way time and time again?

The real failure of modern reform movements lies in the reformers' misunderstanding of the moral principles behind modern government. They suppose that theirs is a fight between morals and no morals, where two opposing parties come to the table on equal terms, appealing to a neutral system of government to hear their cause. In fact, the fight is between two opposing moral systems, each with its own set of ideas about right and wrong. These moral systems do not have equal standing before the state. One of them is the moral system implicit in the very foundation of the state itself.

The moral system behind the machinery of the state is far more powerful than the reformer understands. This moral principle first encourages innovative law and the innovative morality which the law establishes. Reform is a response to such innovation, and an attempt to reverse it. As long as the principle behind the innovation—the engine that drives it—is still there, it will also work to defeat all attempts at reform.

Laws are never created out of thin air. They have a history. They have roots in the legal system. Thus, for example, the "right" to have an abortion has deep roots in the women's movement and the sexual liberation movement. Abortion is a logical consequence of a woman's desire to control her life. Pregnancy and child rearing get in the way of careers and personal goals. Likewise, abortion is a logical next step after both contraception and liberalized divorce laws. These movements have legal roots going back at least as far as the 19th century, when the women's suffrage movement began. The rationalization of killing the fetus is rooted in evolutionary thought. This first required the teaching of evolution in public schools, which became widespread in the 50's and 60's. That, in turn, required public schools to teach it in, which date back to the nineteenth century.

Since law teaches morals, the undergirding legal precedents which make a new law (or the removal of an old law) possible have already been at work teaching people progressive morality for a long time. The new law is always, in some sense, a logical next step to what is already on the books and accepted as valid law. That a new law would even be proposed, much less put into effect, is a sign that the older laws are successfully acting as tutors in the new morality, that this new morality is being accepted, and people are beginning to reason on the basis of that new morality and to draw new logical conclusions.

When a reformer comes against a new law—enacted or proposed—he is coming against a logic that has been ingrained in people already. To oppose a next step is to oppose the logic that produced it, and attempt to keep that logic from being carried to its conclusions. Yet people have accepted the logic

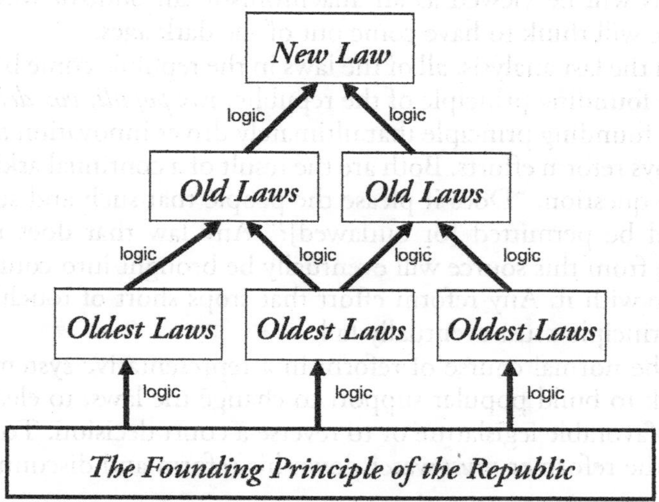

Old laws logically lead to new laws.

already. The older laws have successfully instructed them. It may be only the most progressive who have arrived at the conclusion embodied in a new law, but many, many others are not far behind.

An effective reform effort cannot merely attack the newest law. To be effective, it would have to either (a) uproot all of the logic behind the new law and replace it with a new logic, or (b) use the existing logic to draw a different and better conclusion. Generally speaking, reformers don't do this. When a new law is proposed or passed, they generally just oppose it. Yet even if they successfully oppose it, the logic that produced that law is still there, and will produce similar proposals again and again. So unless the logic behind the law is defeated or redirected, the reformer faces a never-ending battle that he is sure to lose.

At the same time, to attack the logic behind a law is to come against the older laws which have a much broader base of support among the population. The reformer who attempts to do this will be viewed as an anachronism, an oddball whom people will think to have come out of the dark ages.

In the last analysis, all of the laws in the republic come back to the founding principle of the republic, *vox populi, vox dei.* It is this founding principle that ultimately drives innovation and destroys reform efforts. Both are the result of a continual asking of the question, "Does it please the people that such and such should be permitted [or outlawed]?" Any law that does not derive from this source will eventually be brought into conformance with it. Any reform effort that stops short of touching this principle must eventually fail.

The normal course of reform in a representative system is to seek to build popular support to change the laws, to elect a more favorable legislature or to reverse a court decision. To do that, the reformer *must* water down his reform and disconnect

Superficial reform leaves the logic for new laws in place.

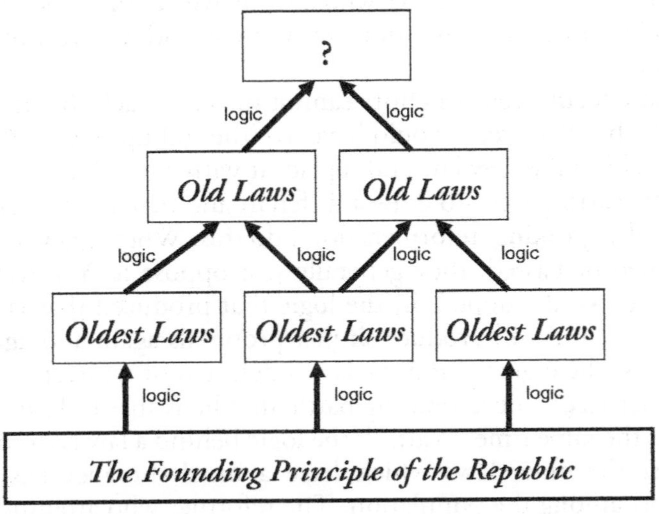

it from its own logical conclusions, because even his supporters have already bought into the morality that the older laws teach, and their inherent logic. If he reaches too far back to the foundations, challenging older laws and older (though still state-created) morality, he will lose supporters. People will get off the bandwagon of reform when reform begins to condemn their morals. Yet watering down the reform leads to the very superficiality that insures defeat. It fails to address the roots of the problem, the logic which is producing objectionable laws and objectionable behavior to begin with.

The pro-life movement is a typical example. The pro-life movement was, back in the 60's and early 70's largely a Roman Catholic movement which was closely tied to the broader birth control issue. Yet today, a pro life advocate who ties abortion to birth control and insists on outlawing birth control along with abortion will lose a tremendous amount of support simply because most adults practice some form of chemical or mechanical birth control and even routinely modify their bodies for that purpose.

Thus all reform faces a no-win situation in a representative republic:

1) To establish meaningful, lasting reform, one must attack the roots of a new moral and a new law that is objectionable. Otherwise the reform is destined to be superficial because older laws establish precedents and creates a logic that leads to the new,

— but —

2) The reformer must focus only on the newest developments which are yet poorly established in order to build majorities sufficient to make a difference in the legislature.

So the very machinery of government insures the defeat of every reform effort. New laws teach new morals which inspire more new laws. The logic of every innovation becomes deeply ingrained into the law and life of the nation and cannot be rooted out. Then that logic inspires new conclusions and new innovation.

As reform fails, those who supported the reform invariably privatize their morals. People who stand up against a particular behavior that they find objectionable don't engage in that behavior themselves. After all, the bottom line on abortion is that if I don't like it, I don't have to get one. If I don't like pornography, I don't have to buy it. If I don't like homosexuality, I don't have to engage in it. So morals foreign to the system become increasingly matters of private belief that can neither be practiced nor even spoken, while the morals engendered by the system itself become established in law.

In the end, even the reformer himself betrays the morality he is trying to establish. By working within the system, the reformer is implicitly accepting the system and its moral principle. He accepts that moral principle as something more fundamental than even the reform. At his best, the reformer is still only submitting the moral which he is concerned about to the voice of the people for ratification, in the form of a changed law, etc. Yet, to the extent that the people do not ratify it, he is willing to let it suffer. If he doesn't get the reform he hopes for, he'll try something else—something more acceptable to the people—and work out a compromise.

In working like this, the reformer confesses that his cause is indeed a matter of personal preference, upon which men may differ, rather than a matter of universal absolutes. These personal preferences are put second to the fundamental morality of the republic.

Unless the reformer is willing to step beyond the system into the realm of the illegal, he is a slave to the system and must inevitably go where it goes. Of course, as soon as the reformer steps into the realm of the illegal, he has the entire force of the state to contend with. That force is for all intents and purposes irresistible, and the mere reformer who faces off against it must invariably become a martyr. The conspicuous absence of martyrs in modern society testifies to the effectiveness with which the state's law tutors even the reticent into its morality.

Indeed, many leaders of reform are so well tutored into the morality of the modern state by the work they undertake that they are turned to positively work for the system and its morality. Some become skilled political candidates and hold office. While they may advance their particular cause a little bit, they advance the state's interests in a thousand other ways while in office, participating on a day to day basis in a lawmaking process that is destroying their own traditional morality. Other reformers attend to peripheral issues in an effort to gain some successes, and effectively work to sanitize the new morality and make it acceptable. For example, pro-lifers often inadvertently work to make abortion more acceptable by attacking gruesome procedures like partial birth abortion or unsafe clinics. The result is more acceptable procedures, and clean state-regulated clinics . . . and an abortion protocol that is more acceptable to the general public and thus harder to get rid of.

CHAPTER 7

The Bottom Line

In the end, the issue we must face is quite simple. The question is, what makes any action wrong? Because man says it is wrong? Or because God says so?

Scripturally, the answer is God. Even if God's determinations of good and evil appear arbitrary, they are true and must be obeyed because they are God's. He is the final judge of the world, and so He has the power to say what is wrong—what He will punish and how.

On the other hand, the moral principle of the modern state is that man determines what is right and wrong. His will is law. Every assertion of right and wrong made by men or gods must be submitted to the system established for making law to validate it. Unless it obtains such validation, it carries no authority. The state's courts will not pay heed to it.

There can be no compromise between these two foundational moral principles. *It is essential to understand this.*

On the one hand, one cannot introduce human lawmaking power to the scriptural principle without overthrowing the very foundation of the scriptures. The scriptures themselves command that we may not add to or take away from God's commandments:

> "Ye shall not add unto the word which I command you, neither shall ye diminish ought from it, that ye may keep the commandments of the LORD your God which I command you."—*Deuteronomy 4:2*

If we do, we've already *broken* the commandment. If we argue that we must reject God's word on one point because we find it objectionable, or unenlightened, or archaic, or because we just don't understand it, then we establish a new principle higher than "Thus saith the LORD". Once such a principle is allowed, where does it stop? The new principle can be used to systematically annul the whole of scripture. There is no longer a higher principle to stop us from doing so, until we are come to a place where man makes all his laws, and God's laws are eliminated.

"if thou judge the law, thou art not a doer of the law"—*James 4:11*

Likewise, one cannot introduce one absolute truth from scripture into the system of the modern state without overthrowing it to the core. To do so is to say there is an absolute higher than any law man can make. There is an absolute principle of right and wrong that no legislature can overturn, that no constitutional amendment can annul. Yet if that admission is made, where is one to stop? If we once admit that murder is absolutely wrong and must be punished as God commands, regardless of what man may think, or what the majority of lawmakers say, then what is to stop the same admission for adultery, and so on? Accept the absolute authority of scripture on one point and there is no principle to keep it from being accepted on all points. The logical conclusion is Deuteronomy 4:2, and the "right" of the people to have the laws of their choice is no more and the republic is dissolved.

One or the other moral principle must dominate, and the subservient principle will be systematically eradicated. The nature of law, as both a statement of morality and a teacher of morality insures this process.

Since the year 1075 when Pope Gregory VII issued his deeply controversial Papal Dictate declaring the Pope to be inerrant and claiming a lawmaking power to himself, mankind has been systematically working out the moral principles of his own lawmaking power, and setting God's laws aside. We have gone very far down this road in the course of the centuries, and the pace at which man has sought to establish his own absolute lawmaking power has accelerated geometrically with the passage of time.

This course cannot be altered as long as the basic values of a representative republic are affirmed. All of the reforms ever attempted from within the system are children of the system. They affirm the system and depend upon the system. They can be nothing more than a child of the system, and not absolute in any proper sense. In the end, the moral principle of the system will reject its bastard children. The marriage of foreign morals with democratic principles will be put to naught, and only the internal morality of the system itself will stand.

It is essential that you and I come to terms with this fact. Refuse to, and everything you ever do will be swallowed up as vanity, and the freight train of the modern state will destroy you and your family and everything you've ever worked for. The only remedy—*the only one*—is to lay an axe to the root of the modern system of government. The moral principle of representative government must be done away with and replaced with the alternative principle of scripture. Such a change *must* come from outside the system. No true change can come from within the framework of the state. The thought doesn't even make sense. To reform the law of the modern state by working for majorities and electing candidates who will make new laws is to fundamentally assent to the very legal principle that has to change . . . that there is no right or wrong apart from what a majority agrees to. We cannot merely ask the legislature to make some new law to make the state better or more to our liking. That is still part of the system. We must ask the legislature to *disband and go home and stay home.* We must establish a new principle of government and a new government to go with it . . . and we must get rid of the present government to make way for the new. Unless and until we do, Christian morality and God's determinations of right and wrong will be rooted up and put away, and God's people will be run out of God's world.

This is revolution though. A total challenge to the moral and legal principle of the establishment. A *new* legal principle with a *new* moral principle behind it. Yet it is absolutely necessary—a logical necessity—if one wants to assert even the simplest truth as an absolute in the modern world. If you are willing to say "Abortion is immoral because Exodus 21:22-25 says so, and it doesn't matter whether anyone agrees" then either you are a revolutionary or a liar. Either you'll stick to this statement or you'll submit to the will of the majority when they vote Exodus 21 out. If you're willing to say "Homosexuality is wrong because Leviticus 20:13 says so," or "Adultery is immoral because Deuteronomy 22:22 says so," etc., etc., etc. . . . in short, if you are willing to assert *any* moral on the basis of scripture, and if you hold it as a higher truth than majority rule, you've already crossed the line of revolution. You may only be coming to realize it as you read this, but revolution is indeed the logical conclusion of such thinking.

This challenge to the system may be totally revolutionary. It may be deeply radical. It may strike at the very heart of everything the modern state is and does. Yet to the simple believer, it is but a modest assertion. After all, *why shouldn't God's assertions of right and wrong be hallowed*, and established for what they are—moral absolutes which no man has the authority to alter? Furthermore, *what business does man have making laws to punish men for actions that God does not condemn as morally wrong?* or for permitting what God has condemned and commanded to be punished? *These are modest assertions*, but wholly unacceptable to the tyrants of modern statecraft. Thus, total confrontation and revolution are the *only* answer.

*

CHAPTER 8

Why Everything Must Go

A godly revolution must necessarily wipe away all of the civil laws of the modern state. The state has, with time, completely twisted all of God's laws into something else. Thus, not only do the foundational principles behind the law have to go, all of the individual laws have to go too. If any of man's laws were to remain, they would continue to tutor men in ungodliness.

Take, for example, modern laws for the road—speed limits, stop lights, licenses, etc. These are laws created by men for the safety of everyone driving on the road. Compare these laws with God's law. His law requires that if one damages someone's property, he pay for the damages. If one injures someone he pays their medical bills, and if they cannot be healed, he is liable to have the same injury inflicted on himself. If one kills someone, he is liable to be killed or confined to a refuge city.

The state's laws do not focus on actual damage or injury. They are technical. Were you going the speed limit? Did you run a red light? Is your license or your insurance expired? Such laws do not teach the individual to have any real concern for his neighbor when driving down the road. They teach him to have a concern for the state, and the state's policeman. Where there are speed limits, people are very careful to think about them and to exceed them only to the extent that they can without getting a ticket. Yet they tend to not think of being careful of their neighbor at the same time. It is up to the state to establish speed limits, to decide where stop lights need to be, etc. Thus the driver considers whether his behavior is *legal*, and not whether it is *safe*. With mandatory insurance, he is almost completely relieved of his responsibility to his neighbor, as long as he is careful about the state's laws. If he has an accident that is his fault, he leaves decisions about compensating his neighbor to a big corporation whose motives revolve around financial self interest, and never speaks to that neighbor again.

In God's economy, it is up to the driver to decide what a safe speed is, or whether he can safely run a red (or green) light. A community might put speed limit signs or stop signs up, but they only constitute an opinion of what is safe. if someone chooses to ignore them they can—however they must be careful of their neighbors. If a posted speed limit is 45 mph and someone hits a child while going 35 mph, he's still liable for the child's injury or death. He cannot hide behind the law. Under such a government, individuals are forced to consider their neighbor in day to day activities like driving. At once, they have the liberty to drive down the road at 110 mph, and yet they cannot hide real irresponsibility behind a man-made law. Neither can they hide irresponsibility behind a state-created screen of mandatory insurance, etc. Although it would be perfectly legal to carry insurance, insurance could not necessarily protect one from the consequences of an injury inflicted on someone, and it couldn't protect one at all in the event of a death. Even the act of buying insurance—since it is no longer mandatory—can become an act of concern for one's neighbor instead of concern for the state.

Thus even simple and seemingly innocuous laws can tutor men to serve God and love one another, or to serve the state and ignore their neighbors. Indeed, sometimes these routine laws that we have to interact with every day are the most pernicious in tutoring us away from Christ, and from goodness, when they could be most effective . . . simply because we do think about them every day.

It is not only the determinations of right and wrong in the law that lead men to God or fail to. The punishments also have tremendous influence. Let us consider, for example, the law concerning theft, and specifically examining the case of someone sneaking into a house and stealing something. In the state's system of justice, the usual punishment for such a crime is a jail term or some form of probation. Again, such punishment teaches the thief to serve the state and not God, to consider the judge who will sentence him, and not his neighbor. He is only peripherally responsible to his neighbor. If the police recover what was stolen, they will generally return it to its owner, but if not, too bad. The victim is thus faced with a double theft: first by the thief, secondly by the state, which robs him through taxes to pay for the prisons, where the thief is given free room and board for his sin. With the state setting such an example, is it any wonder that the thief goes out and steals again as soon as he is set free?

It is foolish to think that the cynical and renegade outlaw cannot see through the moral charade the state is perpetrating, and that the real law he is being held accountable to is that you can steal whatever you can get away with. He sees the state do it, and he follows its example.

In the meantime, the victim is taught to be vindictive and angry. He cannot get compensation from the thief—never. His only recourse is to seek vengeance at the hand of the state. So he is willing to pay taxes to lock this guy up. He is willing to vote for people who will pass ever harsher laws against theft. Thus, societies have often come to the point where thieves are hanged for stealing items of minimal value, or having their hands chopped off, or being imprisoned for a lifetime under "three strikes you're out" types of legislation. Likewise, they burden criminals with records that dog them all their lives. This is not consideration of one's neighbor. It is not Christlike in any sense.

Godly justice forces the thief to consider the person he is stealing from continually. In the act of stealing, he is at risk of being killed on the spot by his victim. After he has stolen, he may confess and pay a 20% restitution in addition to restoring his neighbor's goods. If he's caught, he must pay twofold. If he destroys the goods or sells them the amount of restitution goes up. Furthermore he his held absolutely liable for his act. If he doesn't have the wherewithal to pay the required restitution, he can be sold into slavery to pay for it. Neither are there any statutes of limitations. Thus, his responsibility to restore is held continually before him after the fact of his theft, and the more he steals, the deeper his responsibility becomes. At the same time, the victim's anger is assuaged by restitution. When paid restitution, he can be willing to forgive a thief, and put away his vindictiveness. Indeed, he has no excuse not to. Thus, men can be restored to one another as well as to God.

In the end, every change made to God's laws is a perversion of His laws that turn men away from loving Him and really loving their neighbor. Every change teaches men to serve false gods and serve the state. All such laws, no matter how innocuous the changes may look, are working against God and must be done away with.

*

CHAPTER 9
Turning the Tide

Very well. It is time to turn the tide. If revolution is imperative then it is time to begin sowing the seeds for a godly revolution in the earth—a revolution that will establish godly government, and a law that will lead men to Christ, rather than engendering such a great backsliding. The old, corrupt legal order must be swept away and an entirely new one put in its place. The future of the world depends on it.

The law of God is the key to this revolution. To simply understand it as the final definition of good and evil has earth shaking implications. In this simple assertion, we find both the moral ground to condemn the present governments of this world and the vision for a new and better kind of government. It can well be a hope and a future for generations to come. God's laws will be a tutor in righteousness for hundreds of years.

Furthermore, simply understanding God's law for what it is—a definition of good and evil—frees the believer from the inane theologies that declare God's law to have been put away and that put man's law in its place. The proper understanding of scriptures like Romans 7:1-6, Romans 13:1-7, and 1 Peter 2:12,13 become clear, and the believer is no longer impotent to stand up to the state. Furthermore, this simple understanding of God's law finally proves to be a terrible sharp sword of truth to rip the cover of respectability off of those who continually compromise the truth away, and a sword to force men to decide whom they will serve, God or the state. Gone is the middle ground of unknowing and indecision.

For our part, we must learn to contend for the truth in a way that men have, frankly, forgotten. They have forgotten that because they have ceased to believe in heaven and hell. It is not only the future of the world that is at stake here, but the eternal destiny of many now living. There are millions upon millions of people alive today—many who proudly claim to be Christians—who have no thought of God's law, who know it not, and who break it every day. They bless those who do evil and scoff and distance themselves from those who seek righteousness. They've been trained by the state and by the preachers of a false church to believe they are righteous. Yet, unless they come under conviction and change, they shall surely stand before the judgement seat of God only to hear Him ask "Why do you call me 'Lord, Lord' and do not the things I say?"

The future belongs to those who will simply accept God's judgements about good and evil as final and work out the logical consequences of that truth, pressing it home to individuals and nations. These will be the founding fathers of countries yet to be born, goodly countries where people are free to serve God and live as they see fit.

Now that we have examined the basic forces driving our society—the moral absolutes—and faced the imperative need for revolution, it but remains to consider how to foster the necessary revolution. This strategy itself derives from a proper understanding of God's law and is the subject of the rest of this book. It is basically a strategy of telling the truth of scripture, and allowing that truth to do what it does best: convict and divide men, freeing those who receive it from debilitating lies, and then bringing those who reject it to judgement.

In short, we may summarize this strategy as follows:

1. Illuminate the future of the world.

On the one hand, people must understand the horrors that await them if the moral absolutes of modern government are carried to their logical conclusion. On the other hand, they must understand that there is an alternative, and that it is an alternative where the truth can prosper, where freedom abounds, and where men can serve God as they see fit.

2. Condemn the modern state for the established rebellion against God that it is.

Vision alone is not sufficient to bring about change. Motivation is required. Specifically, the modern state is not simply one alternative for a government. It is an evil alternative, one which establishes and multiplies sin, and maintains its hold in the earth by sinful means. Those who favor it are co-conspirators in a rebellion against God and are serving the evil one.

3. Liberate those who love truth from the demonic doctrines of a false church.

The modern church has a tremendous negative vision for the future. The vast majority of Christians are expecting only calamity and defeat, the rise of the antichrist and their own defeat. Not only do they have nothing to offer for the future, many of them will positively tear down any hopeful idea for the future in the name of their religion. Likewise, they have a negative moral impetus for change. By twisting the scriptures, they demand that Christians offer unqualified obedience to the state, effectively negating God's law and putting man's law in its place. When the foundations are destroyed, the righteous can do nothing. The foundations of true doctrine must be re-established.

4. Condemn those who equate righteousness with obedience to the state.

Those who hold to this false belief commit a multitude of sins every day. They are not God's people and should not be received as such. They are the minions of hell and children of the false church. They stand with the Pharisees of Christ's day, and the papists of the reformation. They must either repent or be damned.

*

CHAPTER 10

How Truth Works

It would be of little more than academic interest to ponder the course of a godly revolution through to the end. Although revolutions have a way of becoming serious very quickly, it may take a generation to start it and a generation to bring it to completion. There is no telling what circumstances might alter its course in that span of time. None the less, it is clearly time to *initiate* a revolution. Under the tutelage of the state and its evil legal system, true faith is rapidly fading. Western Europe is most advanced in its atheism, and the rest of the first and second world countries are following close behind. Even the third world has been deeply compromised. To sit around and wait quietly for people to wake up on their own would be a fatal mistake. They aren't waking up—the great trend of our age is that they are *going to sleep*. Unless someone takes the initiative to wake them up, they will only continue to go to sleep.

This backsliding can only be reversed by a proper application of truth. For truth to be effective, though, the revolutionary must have a completely different attitude toward it than modern man does. This different attitude begins with a better understanding.

BELIEF, TRUTH AND PREFERENCE

Let us first define some terms which modern man twists for his own purposes.

Truth consists of objective facts. True things are true because they *are*, and not because anybody knows them or believes them. No one in the world may believe something is true, but if it is true, this lack of support makes it no less true. Certainly, there can be truths which are beyond our finite ability to ascertain. Likewise there are truths which we may be unwilling to accept for a variety of reasons, and truths that it may be imprudent to confess.

Thus, for example, three centuries ago no one knew that neutrons existed. The fact that no one knew about them made them no less real. Likewise, people may debate the existence of God now because He hides Himself, but no one will debate it when all is said and done.

Sincerely held ***belief*** consists of convictions about what is true. Such beliefs can be about anything, be it philosophical or theological, mathematical, scientific or political. They can be so simple that all but the most foolish will affirm or deny them instantly, or so complex that few will ever truly understand them.

Being convictions, beliefs are not negotiable. One cannot be forced into or bribed out of any truly held belief. Someone can put a gun to my head and force me to say "2+2=5", and even force me to trade everything I own away on that basis, but he can never thereby force me to truly believe 2+2=5. If someone gives me 5 for 2+2, I may verbally assent to the idea that 2+2=5, for the sake of the gain I get from it, but if I even recognize that gain is involved, it proves I didn't really believe, and instead took advantage of another's stupidity.

Of course, this does not mean that men do not change their beliefs. Although one cannot force oneself to change his beliefs, he can change if faced with sensible truths that disprove old beliefs and affirm new ones.

Men can and often do believe things that are not true. Clearly, people often believe lies—and believe them with all their heart. So just because people believe something—even if very many people believe it—it doesn't mean it is true.

Likewise, real beliefs are always discerned by deeds and not words. Some people, for example, may say they believe 2+2=5, but if everyone comes to such a person offering them two

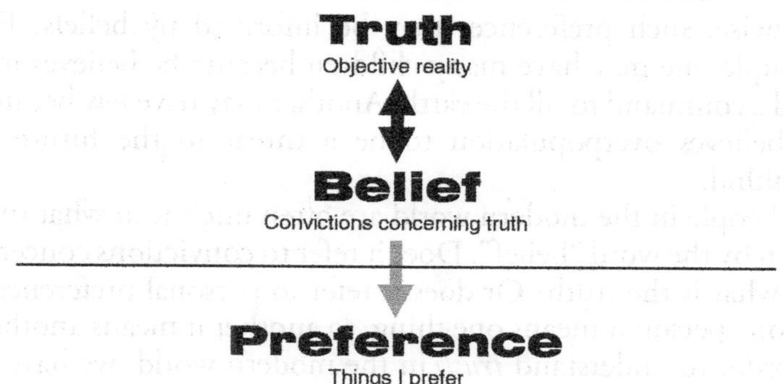

two-ounce gold bars for a five ounce gold bar, that person will usually prove that they don't really believe 2+2=5. They live their real, day to day life by 2+2=4.

Belief has a tendency to fill in the gaps concerning the truth that simple observation cannot ascertain. On the one hand, 2+2=4 is easily verified. On the other, men have tried to logically prove or disprove the existence of God for hundreds of years. Every time a proof is offered, a debunking of that proof is soon to follow. Thus, even very important questions like this can be beyond human ability to scientifically ascertain. Belief fills in the gaps. Few people have seen God face to face. None have yet stood before the great white throne of judgement. Yet many have found sufficient evidence of his hand on their life or His hand in the world, etc., to come to believe in Him. The same could be said of an atheist, who sees in evil and suffering evidence that there is no God, who finds Darwinism a sufficient explanation for how the world came to be what it is, and so convinces himself that there is indeed no God.

Preferences differ from beliefs in that they are things that individuals simply prefer for themselves. One man prefers shoes that tie, another likes slip-on shoes. One wishes to have a large family, another prefers to have only one child. They are not matters of truth, or of belief in the sense of believing in truth. They may involve beliefs in the sense of what someone thinks best for himself, however one man's like is the next's dislike. Likewise, such preferences may be informed by beliefs. For example one may have many children because he believes it is God's command to fill the earth. Another may have few because he believes overpopulation to be a threat to the future of mankind.

People in the modern world are often unclear in what they mean by the word "belief". Does it refer to convictions concerning what is the truth? Or does it refer to personal preferences? To one person it means one thing, to another it means another. In order to understand *truth* in the modern world, we have to be completely clear as to its meaning. As such, I will herein use the word *belief* in the sense of convictions about what is true (even if that "truth" turns out not to be true), and use the word *preference* to denote the other kind of "belief", a personal preference.

Very well, with these definitions in hand, let us examine how truth works.

TRUTH IN THE MODERN AGE

The great absolute of the modern age—that there are no absolutes—is in the last analysis a transformation of all other truths into personal preferences. People no longer call truth "truth". Rather, they call it "belief". However, by calling it that, they do not really mean belief, but rather what we have called preference. In doing so, they effectively eliminate truth in the sense of objective reality from any discussion whatsoever. They show their word game for what it is when they say we must tolerate one another's' "beliefs". This claims an equal footing for all "beliefs", and thus declares them to be mere preferences. *True beliefs, convictions about truth, are never negotiable.* If you think 2+2=5, the kindest thing I can do for you is teach you the truth. If I say it's okay for you to believe what you like about 2+2, I am *not* your friend. I'm affirming the lie you believe and allowing you either to be victimized or turned into a criminal on that basis.

In such an atmosphere, truth becomes a mere currency to bargain with in the political process. Much of modern politics is little more than a game of "I'll tolerate your personal preference if you'll tolerate mine." When preferences clash, compromises are worked out in the legislatures and courts.

Since truth has been reduced to a mere preference, people cease to adopt truths as beliefs because they are convinced they are true. Instead, they adopt supposed truths merely as preferences, because they are convenient or suit their tastes. Such "believers" are insincere. They have ulterior motives for what they say they believe.

Anyone who wishes to faithfully understand truth and belief in this present age must take this widespread insincerity into account. Specifically, when examining beliefs, one *cannot* count them all equal. One has to look at the motives behind popular beliefs. Often their popularity has nothing to do with their correctness. They've been adopted because they are convenient. The motives behind them don't get questioned because that isn't polite in an age where everyone is entitled to believe whatever they wish.

The Church Sells Out

This much we might expect of those who openly deny God and make man the measure of all things. Yet many Christians play exactly the same game. They call the absolute truths of scripture their "beliefs" (meaning preferences) and then sell them out for worldly riches, honor and glory. It is worthwhile to consider some examples of this:

The scriptures demand that men who lie carnally with other men be put to death (Lev 20:13). Yet many Christian leaders advocate some form of tolerance of "alternative lifestyles" instead. In so doing, they suggest that the truth of scripture is merely a private preference that some people choose to live by. In return for such tolerance they buy tolerance for themselves. Denominations don't want, for example, to be forced by the state to ordain homosexual ministers. In the political tradeoff, they buy this privilege with their willingness to adopt tolerance and accept homosexuality in the broader society. They say they shouldn't have to ordain homosexual pastors, but they tell the Christian businessman that he'll have to tolerate sodomites working in his business, etc. Even some big names who speak against homosexuality relatively strongly make open motions of friendship toward those who practice such things merely to avoid the charge of inciting violence (e.g. someone hearing their preaching and taking the scriptures seriously as a result of it).

Again, many Christian leaders are quick to ignore scriptural determinations of right and wrong for the sake of enlarging their congregations and keeping them happy. Thus, for example, they do not condemn usury and refuse to teach the people that it is sin to take usury. Too many people in their congregations (especially the better off ones, who have the most to give) take usury, and the pastors are afraid to offend them by condemning their lifestyles, or appear to be "judgmental" or "intolerant" in any way.

Just so the church buys worldly things—good looks, success, followers, and political power—by trading away the truth for it. Lately, this trend has become virtually a contest among churches in which the most successful are those which have spent the truth most successfully, and those which hold on to it are becoming increasingly labeled as authoritarian cults, etc.

The church is far worse than the world when it trades away the truth, because God ordained the church to be the *keeper* of the truth. The world does not believe the scriptures, but it is faithful to what it believes. Its actions are consistent with its beliefs. It holds those beliefs dear and defends them. The church, though, trades the truth it's been entrusted with away. Rather than living those truths, reasoning them out and defending them, it makes merchandise of them. In the end, the parable of the unjust steward in Luke 16 is a picture of today's church. The steward in times past used his master's riches to build himself up, twisting the truth to enlarge the church's dominion. When it became apparent that it was losing power and people were turning away from it, it began to bargain truth away to the world so that it could have a place in a world that lived by another law than the scripture.

Such comments may appear harsh at first. Surely not all churches are bent on selling out the truth, are they? Of course, the same thing could have been said during the reformation. Surely not every priest was bad, were they? Maybe not, but by the very nature of the system at the time, a few bad men could ruin the whole church, and the bad ones tended to rise to the top and gain an inordinate amount of influence. The power hungry naturally worked to gain high office and consolidate their power. Their evils became established. They could sell out the truth and condone sin with impunity.

Exactly the same condemnation can be leveled at the church today. The church is split into 10,001 denominations and sub-denominations. Bad men have learned to use this division to their selfish advantage, to build big congregations by looting the more faithful churches of members who have been sotted down by the morals of the age. Because the church is so split and irresolute, the *lowest* standard effectively becomes the standard of the church as a whole. Just as a line of infantry is only as strong as its weakest point, the church is only as strong as the worst pastor. If one part of the line runs for cowardice, the battle is lost. If ninety eight churches condemn divorce and one does not, then any time some Christian wants a divorce, he can go to the state's courts and get it, and then join a church that permits it. He takes not only his body there, but his money as well. So the church that condemns divorce loses members and funding, and perhaps closes its doors. The church that permits it grows big, strong and beautiful. Perhaps it grows big and splits, and now it's two churches, then another pastor sees its success and emulates it. So it becomes three churches, etc. In the end, immoral churches have a natural advantage.

Thus, to speak of the church as a whole in such disparaging terms is not amiss now, any more than it was during the reformation. Evil men have learned how to exploit the present organization of the church (or should I say, disorganization) and rise to the top.

THE POWER OF TRUTH

It is little wonder that scriptural truth is not prospering in present day society. How can it, when it is dependent on those who are ready to sell it out at a moment's notice? How can it, when most of the church believes in moral relativism even more deeply than rough sinners, and jettisons its supposed moral absolutes as soon as it sees an opportunity for worldly profit? Certainly, truth can never fare well in such hands. That's not because truth is ineffective though, but because her keepers are unfaithful.

We've got to get this through our heads. The harlot church is the biggest enemy of the truth, not the state, not worldly society. She has drugged people with false doctrines. These doctrines war against the truth and blind men's eyes to it, so that they reject the truth when they hear it. Rather than condemning an ungodly state, the harlot church sanctifies it and puts men under its total authority. Thus, the very people who would be expected to be most inclined to a godly country will in fact reject it out of hand and war against it more violently than anyone. They'll be the first to say "Oh, God's law is not for today", "We must obey the state" and "Revolution is immoral". All of these are knee-jerk reactions that they've been indoctrinated into, based not on an honest understanding of scriptures but on convenient traditions of men that excuse their responsibility to stand up for truth.

Truth can *never* have power in such hands. It can *never* prosper. The solution is to take the truth out of these unfaithful hands.

> ***Revolution shakes the world when the word of God is liberated from the traditional authority of the church.***
>
> —Martin Luther

The real power of truth lies in its ability to create division and bring judgement among those who claim to be righteous. Truth, by its very nature *divides* men. The scripture, which is the truth, is described as a sword, an instrument that divides (Heb 4:12). Jesus said he was the way, the truth and the life (John 14:6), but that he did not come to bring peace, but to bring fire and a sword (Luke 12:49)—to bring division between father and son, mother and daughter and brother and brother (Luke 12:53). Heavenly truth divides men *because many men love darkness* and not light, and prefer to live in darkness, not light. Thus they reject the truth and war against it.

The knowledge of truth also brings judgement upon those who refuse to obey it. Jesus said

> "And that servant, which knew his lord's will, and prepared not himself, neither did according to his will, shall be beaten with many stripes. But he that knew not, and did not commit things worthy of stripes, shall be beaten with few stripes. For unto whomsoever much is given, of him shall much be required, and to whom men have committed much, of him they will ask the more."—*Luke 12:47,48*

Simply put, if one *knows* the truth and doesn't heed it, he is deserving of *many* stripes, whereas one who *doesn't know* deserves only a *few* stripes.

Thus, making the truth known separates God's sheep from the swine that are hiding in the sheepfold, and brings judgement and destruction on the disobedient. Knowledge of the truth will result in either obedience and blessing, or disobedience and severe judgement. God holds men accountable for what they know:

> "Therefore to him that knoweth to do good, and doeth it not, to him it is sin."—*James 4:17*

Widespread ignorance, on the other hand, preserves the status quo and permits even the righteous to drown in a sea of confusion.

So the revolutionary must not make truth known in the polite, compromising way of the religious leaders of this age, who merely proclaim the truth in preparation for selling it out, even as Eve proclaimed the truth (and a little more) to the serpent. Rather, the truth should be proclaimed *with an eye toward creating division, conflict and judgement.* Yes, ***intention-***

ally. That is not mean-spirited or overly contentious. It is simply recognizing the proper function of truth in society and allowing it to so function, rather than frustrating it.

In short, the work of revolution is the work of truth. The revolutionary must be a truth teller. His work of telling the truth is the work of creating division and bringing those who refuse the truth to drink the cup of judgement.

STRATEGIC TRUTH

To bring about lasting political and social change, not all truths have equal importance. Widely accepted truths like 2+2=4 are important enough to holding economies together and everything else. Yet since they are already almost universally accepted, we could write reams of books about them and it would do nothing to change anything. Other truths may not be widely accepted, for example, the doctrine that women should wear head coverings while praying or prophesying (1 Cor 11:5,6), yet working toward their wide acceptance would have a minimal and very indirect effect upon society at large (except possibly to drive women out of the churches).

Certain truths, however, have strategic value. If they were to gain acceptance, they would pull the rug of legitimacy out from under long standing institutions, rendering those institutions unacceptable and providing the impetus for large scale change. They can do that because they cut to the core of the inherent evil of those institutions. Such change will make way for the acceptance of many more truths, and further and deeper reform.

Martin Luther's "the just shall live by faith" was just such a strategic truth. If man could obtain forgiveness and favor directly from God, then he didn't have to buy it from the church. And so of what avail were the church's threats? If he *couldn't* buy grace from the Pope, then he had to live in such a manner as to please God according to the scriptures. This truth created a clear, sharp division on two counts:

1. It undercut the spiritual power of the papacy to open and close heaven for the people, effectively annulling the pope's moral power on earth as well as heaven.

2. It forced people to consider their own salvation, because it could not be gotten by good works or bought from the church. In particular, they were not Christians just because they had been baptized by the church and stayed in the good graces of the church.

Men of conscience had to decide, and either follow the papists, or join the reformation.

Although our situation today is different than what the reformers faced 500 years ago, a strategic truth must be capable of condemning the moral principle by which men live at both an institutional level and a personal level. It must be capable of annulling the state's moral authority, and causing people to question whether the state is leading them to salvation or barring the doors of heaven.

As such a truth does its work in society, it effectively raises the great moral questions which only revolution can resolve. Once such moral questions become burning issues, revolution is at the doorstep.

The proper understanding of God's law as the final determination of right and wrong is the strategic truth necessary to bring such moral questions to the fore. It both obliterates the state's moral authority and forces men of conscience to see that the state's laws are not merely "derived from" God's law, but stand in opposition to it, and to merely permit laws to exist contrary to God's law is to assent to a bountiful harvest of souls for hell. Such laws deceive the unknowing into trusting in a false righteousness that puts self on the throne and pays mere lip service to God.

*

CHAPTER 11

Demonic Doctrines

Obviously, one could not expect too many atheists to back a proposal for a government founded according to a biblical prescription. Non-believers may flock to a Christianity that shows some real faith and determination, even as they have in the past, in the days of the martyrs. However, that cannot happen until a real division has already taken place. That division must start in the church. The first support for revolution must come from the ranks of Christians. Only here will one find people willing to hear the word of God and obey it.

However, most Christians don't really want to even consider revolution as an option, because they have been drugged to sleep with demonic doctrines.

Here then is a paradox: Men of the world will resort to revolution, churchmen will not. Yet we have to look to Christians for the beginnings of the revolution. Of course, if this paradox did not exist, we would probably have had a revolution a long time ago. Demonic doctrines stand in the way—the same doctrines which have disempowered the church to begin with, and allowed the state to triumph in modern times.

In particular, there are two doctrines that have done a great deal toward handing the sheep of God over to the state for slaughter. Let's consider them briefly here, comment on them, and then analyze them in the next two chapters in the light of the truth and learn how to challenge them.

DOCTRINE #1: CONCERNING THE LAW

Most Christians are inclined to reject the idea of revolution because they have been taught by the church to render virtually unqualified obedience to the state. Many ministers today say that God's law was done away with by Christ, and interpret Romans 13 and similar scriptures to demand virtually unqualified obedience to man's laws. This doctrine is appealing to many people because they don't want to be held accountable to God's laws, and they don't want to run the risk of punishment for civil disobedience.

Certainly, people don't profess this doctrine because they've carefully researched the scripture and prayed about it. They profess it because it's convenient. It excuses them from their responsibilities and turns their disdain for truth into a virtue.

DOCTRINE #2: THE END TIMES

Next, the vast majority of Christians have an eschatology of defeat. They believe that in the end the enemies of God will triumph on the earth, and Christianity will be routed out and defeated. Only a magnificent supernatural intervention will establish God's kingdom and destroy the enemy. Apart from this, the enemy must inevitably triumph.

In this age in which the faith is suffering greatly, people who believe this doctrine take it one step further and insist that these are *those* last days. That belief, in combination with their expectation of defeat excuses all of the evil that has happened and is happening. It is the will of God, and who can thwart that? More importantly, the great backsliding is *not* the church's fault and *not* their fault.

This, too, is a doctrine of convenience. People don't believe it because they understand the prophetic scriptures so well, but because it excuses their indolence and their continuing defeat in this life. Again, it turns their vices into virtue.

CHALLENGING THESE DOCTRINES

Such doctrines must be challenged with the truth. Obviously, however, merely holding out the truth as one opinion among many will not achieve the desired result. In the 10,001 different denominations of modern Christianity, there are already churches who hold more or less correct ideas concerning these subjects and they are, frankly, small unpopular churches. Following in their footsteps will at best create a small, unpopular movement that succeeds at nothing.

The key to a different result lies in recognizing that these doctrines are popular not because of intellectual superiority or because they are an accurate representation of spiritual truth, but because they excuse sin and irresponsibility. They are not *causes* of false religion, but *effects*. They grew up to excuse sin and irresponsibility. That is their real purpose, and it explains how they came about.

These doctrines can certainly impede people from coming to the truth. Those who sincerely care about truth may not depart from error unless they hear the truth and have something to fight the error with. At the same time, there are many in the churches that cling to lies because they prefer them. Such as these will not depart from their lies just because they hear the truth. We cannot expect them to. The best we can really hope for is a division. Those that care for the truth will listen to it if they hear it clearly. They will understand why men hold such doctrines, and reject both the doctrines and the men who hold them. So the point is not to win a majority, but to find a minority who will believe the truth.

In the church, the bottom line is salvation. Who has the keys to heaven and hell? God, of course.[1] In the end, He decides who shall go to heaven, and who shall go to hell. Yet, as the keeper of God's word, the church holds out to all the world the conditions of salvation. Thus, by appearances, the church has

1 Revelation 3:7

the keys to heaven and hell. The church teaches men what they must do to be saved. From her they learn the bottom line. Everything else is merely a matter of opinion, or an option. This is why demonic doctrines such as we have discussed are such a problem. They are not understood as essential to salvation. You can have your own opinions on them and still go to heaven. They are just personal preferences. So *why not* hold opinions that are also convenient? If they're truly optional, then there is no motivation from heaven not to choose what's convenient. And there's plenty of practical motivation from the world to take the convenient path.

The keys to heaven and hell must be taken from the church and returned to God. What does it take to be saved? Modern Christianity is leading millions of people astray. It minimalizes the faith by reducing it to praying a prayer "asking Jesus to come into your heart" or "asking Jesus to be your savior", and then continuing to "believe in Jesus" and coming to church with a smile on your face. *Is that all it really takes?*

Is it really true that it doesn't matter what you believe about any variety of issues, including the validity of God's law today, and including the end times?

Or do false beliefs held to in the face of the truth really reveal an evil heart? Do they really point out the fact that people who hold them are only paying lip service to God? That they are really using religion as a cloak to cover their evil?

What indeed shall we say of Christians who don't keep a sharp lookout for sin in their lives, who shirk their responsibility to hear the truth and obey it? What shall we say of those who, upon hearing the truth, make excuses *not* to obey it? Whether we're talking about people who take their pregnant daughters to the abortion clinic to avoid the embarrassment of a bastard child, or those who divorce and remarry because they're at odds with their spouse, those who send their children to public schools to be indoctrinated in worldliness, or women who won't wear a head covering, it's all the same thing in the end: an utter unconcern for the truth.

This is not an isolated phenomenon. It's well nigh universal. Go into any church and you will find it among the leaders. It takes no great intellect to quickly find out where churches prefer their traditions over the scripture. Confront the leadership on it, and watch them reason the truth away for the sake of their tradition.

How can such as these be called children of the Truth? Yet if Jesus called himself the Truth, how can they be called His?? They aren't. They're goats among the sheep. They're following the broad way of Matthew 7:13 that leads to destruction.

This false religion which passes as true faith in the modern age is no different than the Talmudic Judaism of the Pharisees in Jesus' day or the Catholic superstitionism of 500 years ago. It is an adulterated religion that rejects truth for tradition. It has become entrenched not because it is right, *but because it is exactly aligned with the lies which the modern state has established as the great absolute truth of the age.* Modern Christians don't care for truth or God's laws as particular truths because "there are no absolutes" and all truths are therefore reduced to preferences. As such, truth is optional, and churchmen think they can believe whatever they want.

In other words, *these false doctrines do indeed betray an evil heart.* The truth is that the very people who hold such doctrines are leaders in the modern apostasy. Rather than taking the truth of God out of the church to the lost and dying, they're taking the lies of the enemy and setting them up in the church.

Throughout history, there have always been two bodies in one church, the harlot and the virgin bride. One has sold out to the world and worshipped false gods, the other that has kept itself pure. It is difficult to conceive of a deeper selling out than the harlot of this age has accomplished. Her members are being led lockstep into oblivion. They're surrendering their morals wholesale, leaving the churches, and their children are turning into the children of hell. The righteous have to come out of this harlot and reject her and her demonic doctrines or they will be swept away with her. Such an end is simply a logical necessity, just as the end of the modern state is a logical necessity—an outworking of the principle behind it.

CHAPTER 12

A Sorry Excuse for a Lukewarm Life

Rather than confronting modern man in his sins, many preachers condone those sins and mix up the definitions of right and wrong to confuse and silence the righteous. They do it by confusing our responsibilities to God and man, as defined in God's law and man's law. First, they say something to the effect that God's law has passed away, or that we are no longer responsible to keep it. Then they take Romans 13 and tell people that they must keep man's law.

These preachers claim that man, and not God, is the practical determiner of good and evil. It is amazing that such a blatant espousal of Adam's sin could gain widespread acceptance in the church, but it has. *From a strategic viewpoint, this doctrine rates as the great subversion of truth in our time.* It has made all the would-be defenders of the truth impotent to stop the great backsliding of the age, and turned the average churchman into a leader in the modern rebellion.

In order to properly understand the scriptures, let us first look at how the dragon and his minions came up with such a doctrine.

RIGHT MADE WRONG, WRONG MADE RIGHT

Antichrist preachers generally use scriptures like Romans 7:4 out of context to declare "the law" void for a Christian. They quote "ye also are become dead to the law by the body of Christ." Then they add Galatians 2:16, "a man is not justified by the works of the law, but by the faith of Jesus Christ," and 2:19, "I through the law am dead to the law, that I might live unto God." From these, they reason that a Christian need not obey God's law. He is not required to keep it.

Of course, to assert that there is henceforth to be no law whatsoever would lead to total anarchy in both church and state. The antichrists therefore cannot abandon the law completely. They often cling to some watered-down version of the ten commandments, or to the "law of love" or whatever , as the law for the church. They also admit man as the lawmaker for the broader society. This is generally accomplished on the basis of Romans 13 and 1 Peter 2:13. They quote Paul (Rom 13:1,2), "Let every soul be subject unto the higher powers. For there is no power but of God: the powers that be are ordained of God. Whosoever therefore resisteth the power, resisteth the ordinance of God: and they that resist shall receive to themselves damnation." With this out of context quote they make every ordinance of man into the very ordinance of God. They command unqualified obedience using Peter's "Submit yourselves to every ordinance of men for the Lord's sake." Thus the difficulty of doing away with God's law is taken care of. The resulting vacuum is filled by man's law.

Understand that this teaching has deep roots that go back 1700 years. In the first few centuries AD, Christianity was essentially an outlaw faith. Christians were hunted down and killed, and had nothing to do with lawmaking in the Roman empire. However, when the emperor Constantine ascended the throne of the empire in 311 AD and avowed Christianity, ending the persecution and de-funding all the pagan religions supported by the state, new questions about Christianity, the state and the law began to arise. For the next hundred years, Roman emperors used the law to increase the influence of the church on society. Eventually, under Theodosius (378-395 AD), Christianity became a state-mandated religion. Needless to say, such a change of circumstances brought with it a change of attitude among Christians toward the emperor and the law. Rather than renegades, they became overseers. Here was the beginning of this attitude that the king was to receive unqualified obedience. Even so, it did not come to conscious maturity until Pope Gregory VII issued his infamous Papal Dictate of 1075, declaring the pope to be both infallible and endowed to make "laws suitable to the times". Here, then, was a man seated as the vicar of Christ on earth, and effectively king above all kings. He claimed special grace upon his life as a result. He could not err. As such, if he made a law, that law must be of God . . . it could not possibly be wrong . . . and so men were bound to obey it just as surely as if given by a voice from heaven. Such was the resolution of Romans 13 which became established in the high middle ages.

In the reformation, the protestant church rejected catholic authority. In the face of persecution unto death, reformers appealed to the secular state for protection, a protection which secular rulers (who were anxious to get out from under the authority of the pope) were quite willing to extend. Thus, the church and its members effectively came under a supposedly neutral secular authority. This development led to a theology of unqualified obedience to the state. The unqualified obedience reserved to the pope was transferred to the king. The king was thus understood as the vicar of Christ, with special grace from heaven to legislate. That eventually dissolved in the natural philosophy of the enlightenment and its practical outworking in modern republics. Man's law came to be legitimate because it was "good" in an abstract, philosophical sense. Over the past two centuries, this idea of "good" has achieved its democratic apotheosis, being defined as the greatest good for the greatest number. At each step of the way, theology adapted to the necessity of the times, so that, for all practical purposes, good and evil were defined entirely in terms of man. The modern theology that legitimizes the laws of representative government is essentially democratic. The validity of man's law rests not on a special anointing of God for the lawgiver, but upon the law's benefit to man. That the law should always benefit most men is, of course insured by the machinery of modern representative government. Thus, this theology makes no challenge whatsoever to the modern state, any more than a popish theology challenged the authority of the pope, or the theology of the divine right of kings challenged the prerogatives of the king.

CRACKS IN THE FOUNDATION

With a little reflection, any thinking person can begin to see problems with this modern theory of man's law and God's. It is not a carefully thought out theology because it never developed as a conscious effort to get at the truth. Always, for 1700 years, it has been a theology of convenience that justifies the mighty men of the earth in their sin, and forgives the little men for acquiescing to the mighty. It was first developed by paid minions of king and pope at a time when most people were illiterate and it was illegal for an ordinary person to read the Bible. As such, it never needed to be carefully thought out. Men don't accept it because it is thoughtful and correct, but because it justifies them in committing sins they consider unavoidable.

For example, one has to wonder at the fact that both Peter and Paul were *executed* by the state. Generally people who advocate unqualified obedience to the state do not fall so afoul of it that they end up being executed. Certainly not two. Either they were hypocrites in the extreme or they did *not* command unqualified obedience. We might also wonder that the early Christians who learned their faith directly from the apostles were killed by the thousands for crimes against the state. And the apostle John shows them in a place of honor in heaven, not damnation (Rev 6:9-11).

Where did the martyrdom begin, if not in the book of Acts, when Peter and John refused to obey the council when commanded not to speak or teach in the name of Jesus (Acts 4:18-21)? Simply put, they did not obey (5:40-42) which eventually led to the stoning of Stephen and Peter's own imprisonment, which would have resulted in his death, had an angel not intervened. These chapters do not portray Peter as someone quietly submitting to his rulers.

There are likewise many other examples of disobedience to authority that God blessed in the Bible. We can remember the Hebrew midwives when Pharaoh commanded them to kill the Israelite baby boys. We can remember Shadrach, Meeshach and Abednego, who defied Nebuchadnezzar's order to bow down to his golden statue. God preserved them in the fiery furnace and made them an example of faith and courage to everyone under the sun for ages to come. There is Daniel, who despised King Darius' order and continued to pray to God. There was Moses, who slew an Egyptian beating an Israelite. There was Rahab, who hid spies from her king. There were Deborah, Samson, Gideon, Jepthah and others, who drove off those who subjected their people. There were Elijah and other prophets who stood up to wicked kings. Why, we might ask, were the faithful subject to "cruel mockings and scourgings, bonds and imprisonment", why were they "sawn asunder, and slain with the sword"? Why did they wander about "destitute, afflicted and tormented"?

Then, in more modern times, there is the protestant "rebellion". Every reformer, every prince, and every individual who embraced the reformation, from the 16th century onward has acted in direct disobedience to the pope. Until the time of the reformation, the pope was truly the Christian king of Christian kings. To this day he still claims the due of obedience from all Christians. Yet many of us hold these reformers, and their forerunners, men like John Wycliffe, Jan Hus and many others, to be great men and not infidels or heretics. How can that be, if we truly believe in unqualified obedience to authority? Indeed, does not every protestant who holds the doctrine of unqualified obedience confess that he is damned? After all, if we take such a doctrine seriously, every protestant is a child of rebellion.

If the greatness of great men and women of God so often consists in saying with Peter that they will obey God rather than men, then surely there is more to this question of obedience than antichrist preachers would have us believe. A shallow theology of unqualified obedience seems like a sorry excuse for a lukewarm life.

To get at the truth, we must dig deeper.

THE VALIDITY OF GOD'S LAW

I have already quoted abundant scriptures to the effect that God's commandments are not void, and that indeed whether we keep those commandments or not is God's measuring stick of our love for him. Jesus summed it up thus:

> "If ye love me, keep my commandments."—*John 14:15*

The inverse is also true: if we don't keep his commandments, we don't love him. Of course what "my commandments" are depends on who Jesus is. If he is merely some moral teacher who taught us only that we should love God and love our neighbor, then our responsibility is rather vaguely defined. However, if he is the second person of the Trinity, Yahweh God, then all of God's commandments, Old and New Testament, are "my commandments". We must understand them as details about how to carry out the two great commands of loving God and loving one's neighbor. Thus, for example, we understand that it is not loving one's neighbor to steal from him. Likewise, it is not true repentance or true love to just tell someone you're sorry you stole from them. Scripturally, true repentance involves restitution. So God's commands teach us not just *to* love our neighbor, but *how* to love him. We don't reason it out in our heads and decide it's okay to steal from him because it is harder for a rich man to enter heaven than for a camel to go through the eye of a needle, and we piously say we want our neighbor to get to heaven and being poor will help him. God's commandments are necessary to define good and evil for us.

With this in mind, we can take a new look at scriptures like Romans 7. The key to Romans is to understand that Paul is talking about three different "laws". He speaks of the law which is the commandments of God (v. 12). This law he describes as "holy, just and good" (v. 12) and "spiritual" (v. 14). The second law he speaks of is the law of sin and death (v. 23). This is a much older law, going back to the Garden of Eden and Genesis 2:17. Finally, there is the contrary "law of the Spirit of life in

Christ Jesus" (Rom 8:2), which traces its roots back to the Tree of Life.

Now, what Paul is explaining in Romans 1-8 is how, in man, God's law or commandment does not give life. Rather, because man is bound to the *law of sin*, the commandment only gives men a greater knowledge of their sinfulness. Unless brought out from bondage to the law of sin, God's commandment brings only judgement and death, in as much as we break the commandment and incur judgement. Only in an identification with Christ in his death and resurrection (Rom 6:6-8, 7:4) and an assumption of a new life *in Him* is the believer freed from the law of sin and reborn into the law of life (Rom 8:2).

Throughout all of Paul's discussion in Romans, though, he implicitly assumes that sin exists, that there is such a thing as righteousness and unrighteousness, and that these are absolutes that transcend the *giving* of the law by Moses. In other words, good and evil, right and wrong exist independently of the giving of the law. The giving of the law only clarifies our understanding of good and evil and magnifies our responsibility for our sin. To whom much is given, much is required. Thus sin, by the commandment, becomes exceedingly sinful (7:13). No longer can we beg ignorance. *Yet good and evil exist independently of man's knowledge.* These absolutes *are* the commandments or laws of God.

Can the laws of God give life? As mere definitions, no. For the purposes of justification—to gain a right to stand before God—the law only condemns us. Knowledge multiplies our sin and brings greater damnation. The law should drive us to Christ though. In greater knowledge and greater sin, we find a greater need for Him. There we find grace both in the form of propitiation for sin, or substitutionary justification, and God's empowering to live a holy life.

The evidence of that empowering in the believer's life is his conformance to the definitions of the law. Does he live a godly life free from sin? Is he doing the commands of God or excusing himself from them? Is he getting free from sin or falling under even greater bondage to it? A real believer cares about what God says is good and evil. His desire is to be conformed to the image of Christ, the sinless man who kept the law. The commands of God are the measuring stick for one's progress, a light to his eyes, a lamp to his feet. They are the definition of good and evil.

WHAT PAUL AND PETER SAID

Going back to Romans 13, we can begin to see the conflict between God's law and man's if we look a little more carefully. In verses 3 and 4 we read:

> "For rulers are not a terror to ***good*** works, but to the ***evil.*** Wilt thou then not be afraid of the power? do that which is ***good,*** and thou shalt have praise of the same: for he is the minister of God to thee for ***good.*** But if thou do that which is ***evil,*** be afraid: for he beareth not the sword in vain: for he is the minister of God, a revenger to execute wrath upon him that doeth ***evil.***"—*Romans 13:3,4*

Paul predicates his discussion here upon the existence of some concept of good and evil. Who defines good and evil here though? Does the ruler? Or does God? It is no coincidence what follows:

> "Owe no man any thing, but to love one another: for he that loveth another hath fulfilled ***the law.*** For this, Thou shalt not commit adultery, Thou shalt not kill, Thou shalt not steal, Thou shalt not bear false witness, Thou shalt not covet; and if there be any other commandment, it is briefly comprehended in this saying, namely, Thou shalt love thy neighbor as thyself. Love worketh no ill to his neighbour, therefore love is the fulfilling of the law."—*Romans 13:8-10*

Clearly, Paul affirms that *God's* commandments are the specifics of loving one's neighbor and the very definition of good and evil, just as he does implicitly earlier in Romans!

What then, of the ruler who is a terror to *good* works? What of the ruler who is a minister to thee for *evil?* In this modern age it is absurd to suggest that such rulers do not exist. Even in ancient Rome they were plentiful enough.

One must understand Paul as attempting to deal with the overlordship of heathen Rome in the context of his earlier discussion. If

> "... when the Gentiles, which have not the law, do by nature the things contained in the law, these, having not the law, are a law unto themselves, which shew the work of the law written in their hearts, their conscience also bearing witness ..."—*Romans 2:14,15*

then even a Gentile king's laws can be "the ordinance of God" *in as much as they reflect God's law.*

Paul does not directly discuss the *evil* ruler here, though. He *never* commands anyone to put aside their conscience (Rom 13:5) and do what God calls evil for the sake of obedience to man. He says "if thou do that which is *evil,* be afraid". At the very least, Paul's discussion just does not apply to the command to do evil.

We can make a similar comment on 1 Peter 2:13,14. Peter is clearly speaking of "the punishment of *evildoers*" and referring to God's standard of good and evil. In contrast to Paul, Peter does specifically touch on an evil ruler or master, saying

> "this is thankworthy, if a man for conscience toward God endure grief, suffering wrongfully. For what glory is it, if, when ye be buffeted for your faults, ye shall take it patiently? but if, when ye do well, and suffer for it, ye take it patiently, this is acceptable with God"—*1 Peter 2:19,20*

In other words, Peter fully admits the validity of disobedience when obedience would go against one's conscience toward God. Otherwise, *why should he discuss punishment?* One who is obedient does not suffer punishment.

Returning to Romans 13, we can find an even stronger statement against evil rulers if we take a careful look at the language. In verse one, he says there is "no power but of God." Paul implies that if a ruler makes men afraid to do good and commands evil, then he is no true power and no minister of God. His power is dissolved. His authority is abrogated. This is the basic understanding of Romans 13 as regards the pope during the reformation. It is the understanding of the English Revolutionaries and the American Revolutionaries in coming against tyrant kings. Indeed, it is the root of the idea that laws can be invalid by virtue of being unconstitutional (the constitution taking the place of scripture as the ultimate standard of good and evil). It is the foundation for the very idea of "war crimes" and spectacles like the Nuremberg War Trials after World War Two, in which Nazi officials were convicted wholesale of war crimes, and their defense of "obeying orders" was dismissed as inadequate. Thus, ***virtually the whole modern world has come to have an implicit understanding that a man is not responsible to an evil ruler***, when commanded by that evil ruler to do evil. The very legitimacy of his own governments rest on this assertion. Rather he is responsible to God, or to some higher principle of good and evil, to do what is right. Paul's discussion in Romans 13 is the *basis* for these ideas.

In view of this almost universal acknowledgment of a responsibility to higher principle—to God's moral law—which even atheists acknowledge in a deteriorated form—it is the height of fatuous reasoning and pandering to the state for theologians and preachers to claim that Paul commands unqualified obedience in Romans 13. Why not condemn the evildoer, and not his subject, as the scriptures do?

> "Woe unto them that decree unrighteous decrees, and that write grievousness which they have prescribed to turn aside the needy from judgement, and to take away the right from the poor of my people, that widows may be their prey, and that they may rob the fatherless!"—*Isaiah 10:1,2*

DRAWING THE LINE

If one has a responsibility to keep God's law and to obey man's law to the extent that it commands what is good, *and* disobey if it commands evil, then where should one draw the line?

Paul points to conscience as a guide in Romans 13:5:

> Wherefore ye must needs be subject, not only for wrath, but also for conscience sake.—*Romans 13:5*

Yet conscience depends, to some extent, on knowledge. Knowledge of the law of God makes sin exceedingly sinful. If one doesn't *know* that God condemns usury, for example, one's conscience may not bother him to take usury on his bank account. The man who knows his taxes are being used to murder innocent people will feel differently about paying them than the man who does not.

Certainly some kind of laws are necessary for base men who do not know God's commands or even care enough to learn about them, much less obey them. Without some kind of restraint, the worst people would rule over everyone by virtue of sheer terror. Thus, man's laws are better than anarchy, and we can understand that God could ordain them in this context. Yet the more we know about man's law and God's law, the more our consciences are going to bother us. If we only understand that God commands us not to murder, then our conscience may only come into play where murder is involved . . . perhaps if we are "invited" to join a war against our Christian brethren over some matter that hardly concerns us. ***However, when we truly understand that man's law, to the extent that it deviates from God's law, is <u>in contention with</u> God's law, and is working to positively tear down God's laws and tutor men in unrighteousness, then <u>all</u> of man's laws trouble us. They all have a thread of evil running through them, and we cannot stupidly assent to them as if they were good.***

> "He that is not with me is against me."—*Matthew 12:30*

To assent to such laws is to join a rebellion that began with Adam and will continue until the end of this world. So with much wisdom comes much grief.

What Shall We Then Do?

Peter commends suffering wrongful punishment for the sake of conscience toward God:

> "For this is thank worthy, if a man for conscience toward God endure grief, suffering wrongfully. For what glory is it, if, when ye be buffeted for your faults, ye shall take it patiently? but if, when ye do well, and suffer for it, ye take it patiently, this is acceptable with God. For even hereunto were ye called: because Christ also suffered for us, *leaving us an example*, that ye should follow his steps: Who did no sin,

> neither was guile found in his mouth: Who, when he was reviled, reviled not again, when he suffered, he threatened not, but committed himself to him that judgeth righteously."—*1 Peter 2:19-23*

Like Christ, we must finally commit ourselves to Him that judges righteously.

In as much as Peter commends wrongful suffering, though, ***he also commends disobedience for conscience' sake.*** After all, the former is the result of the latter. Yet Peter does not command rebellion or the violent overthrow of the state merely because its laws do not coincide with God's law. The follower of Christ is not to use one man's disobedience to God as an excuse to disobey God himself. Thus, for example, simply because the state violates God's law concerning theft by denying restitution and making the thief a slave to itself by imprisoning him the godly man does not rebel against this law by going out and stealing. God's law still forbids theft, so he cannot steal without offending God. God's law also forbids murder, so the godly man does not go out and start a bloody riot over it. He can rightly condemn man's law for violating God's law, but if he is not himself careful of God's law then such a condemnation is mere hypocrisy.

At the same time we have to recognize the other extreme of blind assent to man's laws is at least as evil. Many modern Christians readily participate in the lawmaking process which puts man's antichrist laws into place. They vote for their candidates and all the various propositions on the ballot every time an election rolls around. So far from suffering for conscience' sake because of these laws, they make others suffer under them. Many today do this out of simple ignorance. They think they are doing God a favor by voting and supporting various candidates. However, to continue to do so once you understand the truth is a very different matter. Likewise, to dumb oneself down and feign ignorance of the truth of what Peter is saying is reprehensible.

Peter's willingness to commend disobedience and suffering for conscience' sake as deeply revolutionary. Essentially, he commends disobedience to one law for the sake of a higher law.

This is *exactly* what revolution entails—the conflict of legal systems and legal principles. In this context, it is easy to understand the tremendous persecutions the early church faced. They were contending against a legal system that had ruled the world for thousands of years. The king, or emperor, was understood to be king by virtue of his own divinity. He was either a god, a descendant of a god, or a god in the making. As such, he was hailed as Lord, the undisputed master of his subjects, by virtue of his divinity. Early Christians refused to hail Caesar as Lord, or sacrifice to him, and went to their deaths for it. In so doing, they refused to acknowledge the fundamental principle of law in the Roman Republic—that Caesar could, as a divine being, make law, or determine good and evil for his subjects. Only God could do that. Only Jesus Christ was Lord. This contention led to a revolution in the fourth century that affected all later kings and kingdoms of Christendom. The king, too, was God's subject, and responsible to Him.

The Conclusion of the Matter

In the end, the anti-christ preachers of this age have turned the plain truth of God's word inside out and upside down. They make man's word the measure of all things, and negate what God says. This overturning is not merely a theological dispute about some hard to understand doctrine. First of all, it is central to biblical faith. Whoever defines good and evil is God. Such a one pretends to open and close heaven with their definitions, admitting the unrighteous into the assembly of the righteous, and condemning the truly righteous. Secondly, the preachers of this age overturn the truth maliciously, with evil motives. *The whole point is to accommodate the culture* and make people feel good about themselves and shield them from the hard decisions that are an inescapable part of true Christian faith. They try to throw wide open the gates of heaven to any law abiding citizen of the republic. Theirs is nothing but a bastard civil religion.

In the end, though, anyone who claims to love God or to love his neighbor, but chooses to define "love" as he sees fit is a liar. The law that defines good and evil also defines the basic standard of love. How then can we say we have God's love for someone when we don't even care enough about what "love" is to learn what God means by it? Indeed, to say that God's law has passed away is to say that God's love—love as He sees it, on His terms—has also passed away. Likewise, anyone who claims to love Christ without the law is also a liar. Jesus could not be the Christ—the sinless lamb of God—apart from God's just law, which defines good and evil and sets the Messiah apart from everyone else. He discerns those who love Him by obedience to His commands, and excludes those who call Him Lord, but do not what He says. To love Him without the law is therefore to love a false Christ.

"Add thou not unto His words, lest He reprove thee, and thou be found a liar."—*Proverbs 30:6*

Chapter 13
Made for Wimps

The popular Christian vision of our future is by and large a rationalization of the modern failure of the church. It is, in every sense, a vision of defeat—the defeat of everything true and good and just, and the victory of raw power.

Some kind of vision for the future—even the end of mankind—is essential for everyone, believer or not. What someone believes about the future of mankind has a direct bearing on what he believes will be the end of all his labors. That, in turn, will determine what he does or does not do. Such a chain of reasoning is inescapable. Simply put, if one sees his work as being of some lasting value, he can do it with a cheerful heart. If he sees it as pointless and useless, then why bother to do it? Even the die hard atheist needs such a vision. So he adopts Darwinism and a vision of the perpetual advance of mankind as his future. Ever growing abundance as the result of technological advance, and the exploration of the stars are his hope. He can work toward that. His life can have some meaning in that context. If he carries his vision too far and embraces the eventual entropic death of the universe, he realizes all is futility in the end and goes crazy.

In this context, the popular eschatology[1] of the church today, in which Christians are irrelevant and defeated, is not merely rationalizing the failure of the church. It is a terrible

1 Eschatology is the study of the end times.

poison that leaves good men powerless to act, and without hope for the future. Their lot is defeat, and all their labors are but in vain.

When Cortez landed in Mexico he was able to conquer toe vast Aztec empire, which commanded hundreds of thousands of warriors, with only a few hundred men. In large part, he succeeded because ancient Aztec legends foretold that white men would come from the east and conquer them. The Aztecs were terrified of Cortez as a result, and every victory he gained only reinforced their faith in their own demise. Their tributaries saw the white men as their sure deliverance and joined them against their Aztec masters. Individuals turned traitor for the sake of their faith in these gods of the east. The defeat of an empire rested on the simple belief that such a defeat was one day inevitable. We should learn a lesson from this.

Let us first take a look at several key elements of this eschatology to see how it embraces the defeat, not only of good men, but of goodness itself. After that, we will go to the scriptures to see just how tenuous such an interpretation of scripture really is.

1. The Church Defeated

The general picture of the end times is one of a collapse of all righteousness, in which the church, which was once great and influential, is overcome and brought to naught. To support this view, scriptures like 1 Timothy 4:1

> "in the latter times some shall depart from the faith, giving heed to seducing spirits, and doctrines of devils"

and 2 Timothy 3:1,2,

> "in the last days perilous times shall come. For men shall be lovers of their own selves, covetous, boasters, proud . . . ."

are cited.

The application of these scriptures to the general decline of the church over the past hundred years or so is generally accepted because people clearly see that the church has declined in influence and fallen from a former glory. It has lost members, and it has been adulterated with false teachings. So far, so good.

The end of this great failure is then said to be the rise of the antichrist and the establishment of the kingdom of ungodliness, the mark of the beast, etc.

The problem here is that this great defeat is generally ascribed to (a) a growing hardness of sinners' hearts, and (b) the will of God. As such, the church has nothing to do with it and can do nothing to stop it. The church has effectively been committed by God to defeat, doomed to a growing irrelevance and ineffectiveness, despite her own goodness.

Without commenting on the truth or falsity of such an assertion, it has to be seen as deeply debilitating. If God has willed for the godly to become impotent and irrelevant to the world they live in, if He has willed that any effort at revival, reform or restoration should fail, if he has willed that our children shall be less inclined to righteousness and more inclined to evil than we are, then there is no hope whatsoever for us and our families. Failure is inevitable. Anything we could do to establish the kingdom of God on earth as it is in heaven *could not* be of God. Indeed, it would be to work against Him. The best we can do is escape with our own soul.

This has to be accounted an horribly destructive world view. What would we say of a soldier who was convinced that if he ever entered battle he would certainly be killed or maimed, and therefore he refused to pick up his gun and fight, but just stood there in battle like a screaming, terrified child. When he did get killed, could we blame it on anything but his neurosis?

2. The Rapture

Most Christians today believe the end of the great apostasy of our age will be a seven year period of tribulation after which Christ returns. However, they also believe they will be "raptured" or taken out of this world before this tribulation occurs. Thus, the sole hope to escape with one's own soul is concretized in this doctrine.

The idea of a rapture is based on 1 Thessalonians 4:17,

> "then we which are alive and remain shall be caught up together with them in the clouds to meet the Lord in the air"

The rapture is an integral part of the modern Christian vision of the end. The modern understanding of the end times makes the great apostasy into no fault of the church. The rapture removes the church from the punishment for it, and vindicates the church as not being responsible for the apostasy—it is a cosmic "not guilty" verdict.

Again, without commenting on the validity of such an eschatology, it cannot escape a thinking man's notice that just as the modern view of the decline of the age makes the righteous impotent, the rapture excuses this impotence and assures the churchman that he will not reap the fruit of his own failure.

3. Israel

Modern expositors of prophecy also make a great deal of a small country in the middle east which has named itself Israel. They count the "end times" to have begun with its establishment in 1948. They believe that the rebuilding of a temple in Jerusalem is a key. They believe that, in the tribulation, this Israel will be God's witness to the world, the church having been taken out.

Once again, the message to the church is one of impotence and irrelevance. The church has nothing to do with and nothing to say about the end times. It's just a non-entity, a spectator. A small socialist country that claims the bloodline of Abraham, however, is of central importance. *They* mark the times and seasons of God. *They* are the keepers of light, the great contenders for the faith in the greatest battle of the faith of all time. And the church is nothing and nowhere.

4. The "Last Days"

Finally, we must consider one other matter which has no real basis in scripture. Many people think that *these* days are the very last days before a virtual destruction of the world in plagues, wars, comets and meteors, etc., and the complete destruction of all evil in the world. After this Jesus Christ will return in the flesh, with power and glory, to establish his millennial kingdom. This kingdom will evidently be populated with resurrected, reincarnated or otherwise glorified bodies, as all believers, Christians and Jews will either be raptured or will have been put to death for refusing the mark of the beast, while all unbelievers will have been wiped out.

This vision of the last days is, once again, a vision of doom. For indeed, if the Christian ever could do anything worthwhile or lasting, here it would certainly be wiped out.

Clearly these four elements of the popular eschatology embrace the utter defeat and reproach of all good and righteous men now living. Many modern Christians count such a scenario a victory. Certainly, if things really went that way, it would be the victory of all the wimps and do-nothings of Christendom. Those who sit back and do nothing but surrender are transformed by this eschatology into God's best *because they refuse to fight*, and by turning and running, they give the world to the devil and hasten the end. Total defeat is the goal, because total defeat is total victory.

Likewise, the wicked are exalted in this topsy-turvy vision of the end. Wicked Jews, who are known the world over for their undying hatred of Christ, become God's favorites. The ungodly—the beast and his crew—successfully take over and rule the world.

Worse, though, this eschatology becomes the victory of the principle of evil over God himself. First, goodness is punished with total impotence. There is no worse punishment possible. Vanity is the great curse of a life apart from God. Everything one does is of no consequence in the end. It is the great lament of the Preacher of Ecclesiastes. It is the horror of hell. It is the sieve of the nations. Only in Christ can we do anything of any lasting value. Even great tyrants understand this much and consign men to labor camps where they are forced to perform vain tasks, rather than just killing them. *Within the context of this punishment,* the undeserved mercy and conversion of God's inveterate enemies is not an act of goodness. It is a horrible act of unfaithfulness—a king making a mockery of his faithful subjects, and embracing those who would stab him in the back.

Ah, yes, everything comes out all right in the end, but at what price? Only at the price of making the foolish virgins wise, making the unfaithful steward right, and vindicating Judas Iscariot. For indeed in this eschatology, one can say that Christians who have been frustrated and ruined in this world have been given eternal life in the next, but if that is so, where is Judas' crime? He could frustrate Jesus in this life, perhaps, but not from an eternal perspective. So Judas sold Jesus to the Jews, who hated him, but Jesus throws the lives of His faithful away and embraces his enemies. The king betrays his faithful subjects and embraces his murderers. Jesus becomes the new Judas, and heaven opens its gates and becomes one with hell. What other paradise could the lawless expect, who fail to understand that heaven is heaven by virtue of its righteousness? Yet what is righteousness, what is faithfulness, if God is not even faithful to His own laws?

DOES THE BIBLE REALLY TEACH SUCH THINGS?

Prophecies are veiled. They always have been, and probably will remain so until they are fulfilled. Few will ever understand them. Ever since such prophecies were recorded, they have been taken and twisted by people to fit their own agendas. The Jews of old wanted a conquering Messiah-king, and the rule of Israel over the world. It was these visions that drove them to revolt against Rome and reap utter destruction. The reformers of the 16th century saw Revelation's prophecies all fulfilled in the Catholic church, and the papists saw them fulfilled in ancient Rome. Amazing how they fit whatever agenda was desired.

Just so, we must understand the popular eschatology of modern times as fitting a purpose. ***It is popular because it panders to what people want.*** They *want* to see the great apostasy of this age as inevitable, *exactly* so they don't have to take responsibility for it. They caused it in the first place. So now they assume a posture of impotence to excuse their incredible unfaithfulness. They believe the righteous shall be impotent because *they* are impotent and assume they are righteous. They believe in the rapture because they don't want to contend for the faith, not now and certainly not in a more hostile environment. They give Israel the central place in their exposition because they'd *rather* be spectators.

However any sane person who examines the scriptures can find a lot of room to question the assertions of modern pop-eschatology.

The idea of the church being defeated despite her righteousness is quite foreign to scripture. The book of Revelation is a book about the judgement of a *reprobate* church. It starts with Christ rebuking the reprobate among the seven churches, and ends with the destruction of the harlot and the restoration of the true bride to the Tree of Life. The church that is defeated is the one that has not been faithful to God, but has willfully served the world and made merchandise of truth. It is the harlot. If these are the end times, then we are living in the age of the prevailing harlot-church, pure and simple. Her judgement is the hope of the righteous. She binds and blinds true believers, and her judgement will be their liberation.

Next, the doctrine of a pre-tribulation rapture is not only vacuous, it is extremely dangerous. It is really not clear what Paul is talking about in 1 Thessalonians 4:17. Pre-tribulation? Post-tribulation? In all likelihood, he's talking about something that is post-millennial, *after* the millennial reign of Christ and in preparation for the great judgement. Those who are devout believers in a pre-tribulation rapture are potentially setting themselves up for a horrible surprise that would be entirely fitting for an apostate church. Just as their belief in this rapture teaches them that they are not responsible for the collapse going on around them, so it teaches them that they needn't worry about submitting to the state and such matters. In particular, since they will be gone before the mark of the beast becomes an issue, they need never worry about taking such a mark. If such beliefs about how the end will come are wrong, though, they could take the mark unwittingly, because they are asleep to the possibility. Then they will wake up to the fact only too late, and find themselves marked and excluded forever from heaven.

As regards the role of a socialist state called Israel in the end times, a number of serious questions have to be considered. Many of the scriptures used to justify such an idea could be debated, and have been debated in many books. Each individual scripture really has to be examined in detail to understand its meaning. For example, Jesus statement about the fig tree in Matthew 24:32 is first of all merely a parable. He says "when you see all these things", speaking not of fig trees, but of various signs he outlined, then the time is near, just as summer is near. Shall we understand this merely as a parable? Next, the interpretation of the fig tree as Israel is highly suspect. After all, the fig tree first appeared in the Garden of Eden, long before there ever was an Israel. More likely it should be interpreted as prosperity, or material possessions, in as much it first clothed Adam and Eve, and so was the first possession of man.

Paul's statement concerning the salvation of Israel (Romans 11:29) comes in the context that "they are not all Israel, which are of Israel" and "they which are the children of the flesh, these are not the children of God, but the children of the promise are counted for the seed" (Romans 9:6-8). So who is Israel? For centuries, Christians have contended that the church is Israel now.[2] Likewise, there has been a long contention, and even an admission by Jews themselves, that the people now called Jews are not of the blood-line of Abraham, Isaac and Jacob. They are Jewish only in the sense that they are more or less believers in traditional Talmudic Judaism, but their blood is that of unrelated peoples that lived in what is now southern Russia, who were converted to Judaism in the Middle Ages.[3] Then there is the mystery of the disappearance of the ten tribes of Israel who

---

2 Charles D. Provan, *The Church is Israel Now,* (1987) Available from Ross House Books, PO Box 158, Vallecito, CA 95251

3 Arthur Koestler, *The Thirteenth Tribe,* (Random House, 1976). A deeply controversial book, over which Koestler was evidently murdered.

were carried off by the Assyrians long before the Babylonians captured Jerusalem. Scriptures appear to speak of a restoration of these tribes which has yet to take place.[4] Then again, perhaps Paul was simply speaking of the tremendous spread of Christianity in Judea before the Romans sacked Jerusalem in 70 AD.[5]

What is the truth? This author does not presume to be an expert at interpreting such prophecies. However, it certainly seems *possible* that the modern day country called Israel may have no prophetic significance whatsoever, being socialist and not theocratic, thus not politically a restoration of Israel, and not the seedline of Israel. One has to remember that at various times in the past, it was believed that Israel was being restored in prophetic fulfillment, only to result in nothing. During the 11th century, and again in the 13th century, the Crusades liberated Jerusalem from the hands of infidel Islam. Jerusalem was once again in the hands of true Israel (the church) after a millennium of ruin and being trodden under foot by the gentiles. Surely *this* was the fulfillment of prophecy! But it wasn't. Are we any better off today, or are modern day Israelis (they do not call themselves Israel*ites*) merely exploiting the scriptures to gain critical military support from the gullible west, so they don't get driven into the sea by the Moslems?

With regards to the last days and the destruction of the earth, one must understand that the coming of Christ in Revelation 19 may be something that happens in a spiritual realm, and the battle described may be a spiritual battle, just as the various beasts of Daniel and the Beast of Revelation represent various spiritual forces. In the millennial kingdom described in Revelation 20, we read that only those who refused the mark of the beast reigned with Christ a thousand years. Yet, such "reigning" may not involve Christ's physical presence at all.

---

4 See, for example, Hosea 1:11, which speaks of a restoration of both Judah and Israel,

5 James Jordan, *The Future of Israel Reconsidered*, available from Biblical Horizons, PO Box 1096, Niceville, Florida 32588.

Indeed, could we not justifiably say that Karl Marx reigned over many nations in the 20th century, even though he died before 1900? So it could be in the prophesied millennial kingdom as well, and Christ could only return physically at the end of that time for the judgement.

Certainly, the millennial kingdom has some scriptural aspects that make it quite different than the popular conception. One of the most important is that it is not universal. We read:

> "And when the thousand years are expired, Satan shall be loosed out of his prison, and shall go out to deceive the nations which are in the four quarters of the earth, Gog and Magog, to gather them together to battle, the number of whom is as the sand of the sea."—*Revelation 20:7,8*

In other words, ***the millennial kingdom is not universal!*** There are still other nations around that apparently do not serve Christ! Such a picture of God's kingdom on earth, though scriptural, is never mentioned in popular accounts of the end, which portray that millennial kingdom as universal. Such a possibility would suggest that these popular accounts fall far and wide of the mark of accuracy.

Realize that there is one whole school of Bible interpretation —the preterists—that relegates all of the prophecies of Revelation to the first century AD. The great tribulation was when Jerusalem was sacked. Nero was the antichrist, Jerusalem and Judaism the whore, etc. While not a popular understanding, it has certain merits, which are beyond the scope of this book to discuss. Then there is the interpretation popular in the Reformation, which declares the Pope the antichrist, Rome Babylon, and the Catholic Church the whore. Certainly it is not wise to ignore such interpretations merely because one does not care to put in the effort to learn a little history.

Finally, one has to consider the persons who were principal in making this modern day eschatology popular. Cyrus I. Scofield, of the famous *Scofield Reference Bible*, for example, appears to have been an opportunist who sought fame, and who was less than concerned for accuracy and truth. He was a former lawyer and politician who styled himself as a Doctor, though he had no degree, and who ingratiated himself with all the scholars of Christendom and adopted tactics to make his work influential.[6] Neither is Scofield alone in his lack of concern for truth. The question begs to be asked: Should a Christian trust such people to interpret prophecy for him?

Needless to say, one does not hear such questions and problems with the modern prophetic interpretations raised in most churches. The mainstream ideas are presented as if they were tried and true fact, and they gain popularity by frequent repetition, *not because they have been weighed and compared with various other ideas and have come forth shining.* The truth is, if they are weighed in the balances, they are found wanting. Anyone who cares to do a little study can discover that for himself.[7] This is merely a theology of convenience, adopted because it encourages sinful man's sinful desires, and adopted intentionally by pastors and people who want to build big churches for show. Thus, the end times as the average modern Christian understands them are little more than a fantasy game to help him escape from reality.

BACK TO EDEN

One of the worst consequences of pop-eschatology is that it makes strong hands limp. It leads to impotence in every area of life, and a morbid resignation to evil. It is not the purpose of this book to lay out a detailed alternative interpretation of prophecy. However, the righteous must understand that they have the power to do good or evil. Years of brainwashing with this dispensational pre-millennial eschatology, and the theology which it produces has left many Christians with some idea that they cannot, and indeed should not, will to do anything.

---

6 Joseph M. Canfield, *The Incredible Scofield and His Book*, (Ross House Books, Vallecito, Calif.:1988).

7 A good place to start might be *The Journal of Christian Reconstruction, Symposium on Eschatology*, Volume 15, Winter, 1998, published by Chalcedon, PO Box 158, Vallecito, Calif. 95251

Human will, they suggest, is evil, and it is best to simply be passive and let God run things. God, they say, is interested in breaking the human will and reducing every man to a sort of machine that just obeys orders day by day, with no thought of where those orders lead. Such thinking is not only totally ruinous, but deeply evil.

Of course, it is impossible *not* to will to do *something* unless one has serious brain damage. Even the person who chooses to lie in bed all day for fear of doing something is doing something. Lying in bed may not be very productive or useful, but it is *something*. Indeed, it is absolutely necessary for men to act. They cannot help it. Furthermore, men can plan and think long term, and carry out long term plans. Neither is such planning evil. It is essential to man's being man.

When God created man, He gave him authority to eat from the fruit of trees. This is not something He gave to the animals. If we take this as merely a natural statement, it means little today. Yet the trees of the Garden hardly sound like natural trees. What, after all, is this Tree of Life, and this Tree of the Knowledge of Good and Evil? Throughout scripture, trees have significance. For example, why should a man be cursed if he is hung on a tree?[8]

The key to what a tree signifies can be found in the original Hebrew language. The word for "tree" in Hebrew is עץ, *getz*. The feminine of this word is עצה, *getzah*, which means to "shut one's eyes", in the sense of receiving bad counsel. The verbal form is יעץ, *yagatz*, which means to purpose, devise, or counsel. Thus, the trees have to do with purposing, devising plans, or taking counsel.

With such insight, the idea of a Tree of the Knowledge of Good and Evil makes perfect sense. Adam and Eve, by eating the fruit of this tree, took the counsel of the serpent and purposed to know good and evil for themselves. Their eyes were

---

8 Deuteronomy 21:22,23

opened to their own power and closed to God. They tried to hide the fact that they had done this by hiding amongst the trees—in a multiplicity of purposes and plans. That, of course, is exactly what every man does. He's too busy with his own plans to come to Christ. When stripped down to essentials, though, he wants to determine good and evil for himself. All his other plans and purposes are just a smoke-screen for this fact.

This is the very difference between man and the animals, too. An animal cannot plan, it cannot purpose in its heart to do something that will take years of planning, work and ingenuity. It can only deal with immediate situations that present itself. It can look for food when it is hungry, sleep when it is tired, etc.

The curse of the tree makes sense in this context, too. It represents a man who is destroyed by his own purposes. He has taken bad counsel to the point that his eyes are closed and he cannot change. Then he is cursed and kept away from salvation.

Likewise, a multitude of scriptures also make better sense in this context. For example, Psalm 1, the man who does not walk in the *counsel* of the ungodly is like a *tree* that brings forth fruit in season, whose leaf does not wither and whatever he *does* prospers. Or in Matthew 7:17-19, Jesus says a good tree brings forth good fruit and a bad tree brings forth bad fruit, speaking of how a man's inward purposes bring forth results. The list goes on and on.

Yet if part of being man is being allowed to partake of the trees, by virtue of considering possibilities, purposing and devising plans, *can he even begin to know God unless he does?* God gave man the trees to eat and called them good. Man must choose *something*, he must do *something*, and in the doing he meets God. The fruit that comes of it will reveal his heart so he can see it, and he can change his plans or purposes, but purpose he must. With wisdom and humility, he can align his purposes with God's purposes for him, and avoid being hung by them, as it were.

Thus, this bizarre doctrine of willing nothing and doing nothing suggests that God's purpose is to turn man into an animal, in as much as the man is ideally to be unable (through lack of use) or unwilling to purpose. His attempts to do so are frustrated and condemned by God. Yet an animal that cannot purpose also cannot incur moral guilt. Moral responsibility goes hand in hand with the ability to purpose. So the man who cannot purpose effectively becomes an amoral being. At this point we come back to modern philosophy and "there are no absolutes", because to an amoral being there really are no absolutes. Indeed, this modern theology has roots deeper than we might have imagined at first!

The conscientious Christian must reject such doctrines. They do not lead to God. They separate man from God. Those who do not will anything can never taste success or failure. They are sterile trees that bear no fruit. Those who will not purpose will never meet Him walking in the cool of the day amidst the trees of the Garden.

REVOLUTION IN OUR TIME

In the end, the righteous need not be burdened with a theology of impotence. God intended man to consider his ways, to pay heed to good counsel, and to purpose and do. That is a major distinction between man and an animal. To surrender it is to surrender one's very humanity.

The scriptures also have much to say about the gradual growth of God's kingdom. The stone that smashes Nebuchadnezzar's statue grows into a mountain that fills the earth. It is a kingdom that will never be destroyed, and that will break in pieces and consume all other kingdoms. The gospel is spread and the nations are discipled. Of the *increase* of Messiah's government and of peace there shall be no end. These prophetic scriptures speak of a process, not a single act.

As such, it is perfectly reasonable for the servant of God to work toward righteous ends, and to work toward establishing God's total kingdom on earth as it is in heaven. Neither is it unreasonable to suggest that one work toward a better principle of government, or that such a government *could* be accounted part of the prophetic fulfillment of the increase of Messiah's government, and perhaps even the coming of the millennium.

After all, we cannot reasonably expect Jesus to come back and stage a world-wide election with Himself and Beelzebub as candidates, or that he will be the acclaimed president-elect of some great representative republic coming down from heaven complete with its legislatures, social programs and fiat money. At the same time, we can in good conscience leave what God will do to God. Whether Christ comes in the millennium as spirit or flesh is up to God, as are so many of the details about the future that pop-eschatology wants to pin down. What we really can be sure of is that if the righteous make prayerful plans and set their hands to the plow and work, and are careful to adopt godly ways, they shall succeed. Their work shall not be in vain. This much is the promise of God:

> "Blessed is the man that walketh not in the counsel of the ungodly, nor standeth in the way of sinners, nor sitteth in the seat of the scornful. But his delight is in the law of the LORD and in his law doth he meditate day and night. And he shall be like a tree planted by the rivers of water, that bringeth forth his fruit in his season, his leaf also shall not wither, and whatsoever he doeth shall prosper."—*Psalm 1:1-3*

CHAPTER 14

The Future of the Modern State

Let us lay aside vain fantasies about the future and turn our attention to the real thing now. The modern state is facing a crisis of legitimacy that has been driving its development for the past several hundred years, and will continue to drive it in the future. This crisis, already the most important force driving the development of the state at present, is accelerating for reasons that are beyond the state's power to control.

In ancient times, kingdoms were legitimate because the king was viewed as divine. He was a god, a child of the gods, or a god in the making. By virtue of his divinity, his word was absolute—it was law. As Christianity became established, this doctrine of legitimacy was supplanted by another. The kingdom was legitimate because God ordained it. God appointed kings who were accountable to the ecclesiastical authority (at least to some extent). Laws were laws because they derived from God's laws. The theology that justified these concepts might have been twisted, but it tied the legitimacy of the state to the faith of the people. The state still had a divine authority. To question that was to question God and court damnation both in this world and the next.

This divine link to legitimacy was broken as a result of the separation of church and state that has grown up in the past 500 years. Although statists may have courted such a separation as a means to freeing themselves from a politicized papacy, they suffered greatly from it by undermining their own basis for legitimacy.

At first, the new basis for legitimacy was simply absolute monarchy, a monarch unaccountable to anyone. A mythology developed around this monarchy that related the the king to Christ and the king's subjects to the bride of Christ. Yet this pseudo-Christian mythology proved hollow and failed to establish a lasting legitimacy for absolute monarchy, while abusive monarchs did much to undermine the legitimacy of the institution as a whole. This led to the secular revolutions of modern times, starting with the English Revolution and the execution of King Charles I.

These revolutions sought another foundation for legitimacy in the voice of the people. The expression of this voice of the people, or *vox populi* was a complex matter as it was resolved in the earlier English and American Revolutions, but it seemed to work. However, when the practical day-to-day needs of the destitute poor became the driving force of the French Revolution, and the revolutionary government tried to resolve these physical and economic needs with politics, it became clear to those who did not already know it from history that the voice of the people could be a monster in disguise. The communist revolutions of the 20th century have only served to make this fact all the more clear. Although the communists learned their lessons well enough, and have become very skilled at exploiting the gut needs of the poor as a ladder to power, they have not done so without completely undermining the idea that the will of the people can legitimize government. Wherever they go, tyranny, oppression and misery follow. Just as the atrocities of the most ardent adherents of absolute monarchy destroyed the legitimacy of absolute monarchy, so the atrocities of the adherents of this modern mythology of legitimacy have virtually wrecked it. Neither does that apply only to communists. Demagogues of all stripes have demonstrated how the voice of the people can be abused to create perverse laws and governments.

Even in countries where the tyrannical side of the *vox populi* has not been fully experienced, growing numbers of people have begun to see their own government as essentially a law unto itself. They can see tyrannical expressions of such government in other countries, and reason out well enough what is possible in their own. They see the general trend that their laws are becoming increasingly arbitrary, no longer serving the interests of a higher ideal of justice. They are merely tools of the powerful to justify themselves. The end result is a cynicism about the government that breeds widespread apathy and undermines the legitimacy of the state.

The logical conclusion of the moral principle behind the modern state is also combining with cynicism to threaten the legitimacy of the state. If there really are no absolutes then obedience to the state's laws is not absolutely necessary. It becomes a practical affair. If it is not likely one will get caught, or if it is not to one's liking to obey, then why do it? There is no moral absolute broken if one does not obey, because there are no moral absolutes.

This philosophical legitimacy crisis is quickly becoming a crisis of survival because technology is also changing the power equation on which the state is based. Individuals and small groups of people have far more power than they ever had in the past. Two hundred years ago, to raze a city required a vast army and months of siege. Today, one man with a small vial of a suitable biological agent can accomplish the same destruction. Wealthy individuals like Saudi millionaire Osama Bin Laden, or Columbian drug lord Pablo Escobar have actually challenged whole nations. At a more benign level, technology is also making it possible for more and more individuals to free themselves from the control of a single government. Many, many people are doing exactly this to avoid taxes, inane laws, and capricious courts. When the months it used to take to travel to another country are reduced to hours, and when one can maintain a virtual presence just about anywhere on earth via telecommunications and the internet, the grip that nations have on individuals—especially the most productive ones—is weakening.

When these technological and philosophical forces are combined, it becomes apparent that the state is going to face a major crisis that could threaten its existence. This looming crisis has not been widely acknowledged yet, but it is becoming a driving force in statecraft.

SERVICES AND CLIENTS

The success of republics over the last couple hundred years has been, in large part, due to their ability to adapt and accommodate forces that might otherwise destroy them. Republics were designed in the 18th century according to the theories of power that applied to the 18th century. At that time, power resided in numbers. Republics accommodate numbers. Majorities and significant minorities, if cohesive, can get their way by virtue of their ability to put one candidate or another into office.

Such a system resolved the fundamental instabilities of an absolute monarchy. Simply put, leaders could be done away with without putting the whole system in jeopardy. No longer did they have to be executed, and their children exiled while rifts of loyalties among the people give dangerous undercurrents to politics. Bad rulers could simply be voted out of office and their bad laws could be reversed.

All states tend to develop power bases by creating services and maintaining clientele for those services. Typically, services are created for the benefit of those who have power. In a republic, the state creates and maintains clientele for an ever-expanding array of services. These services take a variety of forms, all of which have ancient roots and have been adapted to modern conditions. The clientele for various services become vested interests who will staunchly defend the continuation or expansion of the services they use. Thus, as the government, or various power factions within the government, establish services and build client bases, they insure their power. Special interests will support the state, or support their favored party with votes and campaign contributions, not out of any idealism, but because they want the services.

The services which the state supplies to its various clients fall into five categories:

1. Protection from criminals

The state originally protected private individuals from crime for moral reasons, as part of its commission from God. As it has deviated from God's law, however, it has put man at the center. It protects people from crime as a service—a service that has political value.

2. Monetary Payments

The state taxes its subjects and then gives the money to others.[1] In ancient times, money used to go into the coffers of the king and his favorites. Modern republics put money into the pockets of all kinds of special interests. If a significant voting block can be identified that will respond to money, it will be so approached. The government will make direct payments, facilitate loans, manipulate prices of goods and services, or the stock market, etc., etc.

3. Patents

The state grants various individuals and groups special rights or patents to carry on a particular activity or business. In ancient times, a king's favorites, or those who paid appropriate sums to the royal treasury could obtain such grants. Modern republics tend to make these grants in exchange for money, or upon meeting various technical and educational criteria. Thus, for example, one can obtain a business license in exchange for the payment of a "transaction privilege tax", more commonly known as a sales tax. Or one can start a bank provided he complies with the technical rules of the central bank. He can practice medicine provided he's completed the course of instruction at an accredited medical school, and agrees to provide only approved treatments. Effectively, those who agree to serve the state's interests are given patents to carry out an activity, exclud-

1 Printing money is also a form of tax because it robs people through inflation, making their money worth less.

ing the competition of those that will not make such agreements.

4. Legislative favors

Being in possession of the lawmaking prerogative, the state can grant legislative favors to special interests, by permitting one thing or regulating another. Thus, for example, it can create a new client base by giving women the right to vote, or by legalizing homosexuality.

5. Protecting against foreign interests

The state commonly protects its citizens from foreign invasion. It also protects various special interests from foreign interests of other sorts. For example, modern governments typically protect laborers by excluding foreign labor. They exclude or penalize the import of various foreign products with duties and import quotas and embargoes.

When the state creates client bases using these techniques, it does not bolster its legitimacy in any philosophical sense. Practically, though, it gives people reason not to question its legitimacy. It is in their self-interest to keep the government around, so why tear it down? Furthermore, to question the state's legitimacy is to question the legitimacy of the benefits they receive. If those benefits are not legitimate, they are immoral, and the person who receives them is immoral. Thus, the legitimacy of the individual's own life and actions becomes tied into the legitimacy of the state. To question the state's legitimacy is to question one's own legitimacy—something few people are willing to do unless they have strong motivation.

THE BREAKDOWN

This formula for maintaining the state's legitimacy will work only so long as 18th century ideas of power remain operative. As long as the majority can force its will on minorities it can take their money and it can establish privileges for itself and there is little the minority can do about it. If they cannot force their will, though, the state is forced to either return to a philosophical basis for legitimacy (get people to believe in it) or to discard legitimacy and operate on the basis of brute force.

Today individuals do have far more power than they did a century ago, and their power relative to the state is growing day by day. Technology gives people who question the state's legitimacy loopholes to avoid its laws or to attack it. A productive person who is tired of making transfer payments to the state can relocate his business and/or himself offshore. A doctor who wishes to administer a new treatment that has yet to be approved can establish a branch clinic in a more liberal country. A company that wants to use cheap foreign labor just moves offshore. Someone irritated with a legislator's pro-homosexual stand sends him a letter about it, contaminated with a virus that will prove fatal to everyone in his office. Although the state may be expert at accommodating majorities, it is incapable of accommodating every individual. It has neither the means nor the philosophical inclination to do so.

As such, the state's standard formula for maintaining its legitimacy is breaking down. *So what* if the state decides to raise the tax rate for some new program? The people paying the taxes will just flee all the faster, and tax revenues will fall, destroying all of the state's programs. And what happens when the state's attempts to gain the favor of one group with its legislative fiat only angers another group enough to take retribution against the state? The only recourse is to return to the philosophical basis of legitimacy. People will only pay high taxes if they believe in the state in some sense. They will not take retribution only if they believe it is wrong in some sense.

Yet the state's philosophical basis of legitimacy, which is tied into its fundamental moral principle, is self-destructing at the same time that its formulas are failing. In a world without absolutes, the whole idea of legitimacy collapses. Nothing is legitimate or illegitimate, and everyone is basically free to take whatever they can . . . and get away with whatever they can. Such logic applies to both ruler and ruled. Legislators pass whatever laws they will, so long as they are capable of doing it without rousing such voter ire that their office is in doubt in the next election. Citizens have few qualms about taking benefits while at the same time shirking concomitant responsibilities, without ever considering the morality of such actions, simply because morality doesn't have an objective reality any more. All that matters is one's present desires.

It is questionable whether the state can withstand such a double-pronged assault on its legitimacy. Some authors have made a case against it.[2] However, whether it does survive or not, we can be certain that it will *attempt* to survive. The stakes are too high for it to roll over and die quietly. Too much money and power, and too many careers are at stake. It is this attempt to survive that is already driving lawmaking today, and which will propel the state into the future. To understand what the modern state will become in the future, we must understand where these trends will lead.

THE PERSON AND THE STATE

The Latin word *persona* literally means "sounding through" and originally referred to the mask an actor wore in a theater. The mask replaced the actor's face, making him into a different individual, as it were, and yet allowed his voice to sound through it. This language of the theater came to apply in the legal realm in Rome. A Roman citizen was not merely a private individual. He also had a legal personality or *persona.* He had a role to play in the public arena, yet a role where his own voice—his own ideas and desires—could sound through. In this role, the person had both rights and duties. He had taxes to pay, but he had a right to a trial when accused of wrongdoing, etc. Apart from this *persona*, the individual was just a raw man, not part of society or the legal order. He had no rights or duties and was an enemy of society fit only for slavery or death.

---

2 See for example James Dale Davidson & Lord William Rees-Mogg, *The Sovereign Individual*, Simon and Schuster, 1997.

Modern republics have adopted this concept of the legal person. Indeed, it is foundational to their philosophy. Slogans like "all men are created equal" refer to the *persona*, not the natural man. Obviously, natural men are not born equal. One is male, the next is female. One is English, the other Irish. One has genes to make him strong, another to make him smart. Yet, before the law and in their relationship to the state, they are created equal in the republic.[3] Likewise we can see this principle at work in the institution of slavery in some early republics like the United States. A slave had no *persona*, and hence no rights. Thus, the apparent contradiction between slavery and all men being created equal made perfect sense from a legal standpoint.

It is in the *persona*, the legal person, that individuals have standing before the state. By virtue of that *persona* they have rights and responsibilities. Without it, they have no standing. A foreigner coming into a country requires a visa in order to obtain a temporary *persona* in that country. Without it, he is an "illegal alien" subject to deportation or detention without recourse. A foreigner in another country can be lawfully killed in war, etc., and there are no repercussions for his killer because the foreigner has no legal status, no *persona* in the nation staging the attack.

THE STATE'S RESPONSE

Obviously, the state must respond to the tremendous forces coming against it, or cease to exist. That it will respond to them is beyond reasonable doubt. Those whose careers are wrapped up in the political life of the nation consider the continuation of their government to be a necessity beyond discussion. When push comes to shove, most people will agree with them. Anything—even tyranny—is better than anarchy and continual terror. Yet the modern state is philosophically bankrupt. The moral system it engendered—*vox populi, vox dei*—is now de-

3 That is not so in a kingdom that recognizes nobility. It is in such a context that this statement was originally made.

stroying its legitimacy, since there are no absolutes, *including* the state. As such, the state has little choice but to respond to the crisis it is facing with brute force. Other options just aren't available.

The form that this response will take is largely dictated by the threat itself, and where it comes from: large scale crimes committed by individuals.

Clearly, when a nuclear, chemical or biological attack could cost millions of lives and neutralize the state in one day, the price is too high to be content with punishing the criminal after the fact.

For society to simply survive, every effort must be made to stop crimes *before* they are committed. Right now, that "every effort" is practically limited to what people will put up with. If, on the other hand, someone were to successfully perpetrate a biological attack in a major North American or European city and kill a million people, society would change its attitude over night. When the perception of the ordinary man shifts, and he realizes that such possibilities are not science fiction, but real threats that could claim his life next year, next month or next week, he will really begin to demand that every effort be made to protect him. Gone will be any irritation at losing his rights. He will be content to keep his life. At this point the state will really begin to apply all of its resources to stopping crimes before they happen. All of its legislative ability, all of its financial resources, all technology . . . everything possible.

In order to stop real crimes before they happen, the state must extend the concept of crime to the realm of human thought. Then the state must invade the once private realm of thought in every way possible, both in order to control men's thoughts so that they will not commit crimes in the first place, and to discern dangerous thoughts that could lead to crime before they do. And of course, the state must have the authority to deal with dangerous thoughts and the individuals who harbor them. As such, various thoughts will become meta-crimes, if not actual crimes.

To seriously consider this necessity-driven invasion of the thought life of man by a state without morals and where it could lead in the next fifty years is truly horrifying. On the one hand, it leads to a total invasive monitoring of the actions of every individual in an effort to discover evil thoughts behind those actions and stop them before they are turned to action. On the other hand, it leads to an invasion of personal lives and even one's own body in an effort to control thoughts. Really, a tremendous amount of technology exists that could be put to use to both discover and control the individual's thoughts, should people ever decide to use it.

The key to implementing such programs is the *persona*. At the present, doctrines like "all men are created equal" still help us to define the *persona* as a natural right. Every individual born in a nation is bequeathed with a *persona*. He has the rights and responsibilities of citizenship. Forces have already been unleashed to change this fundamental idea. It may not be very long before a naturally born individual does not automatically get a *persona* from the state. Rather, he will have to be reborn in a sense, in an image amenable to the state.

Precedents for such a rebirth already exist in the many licensing programs that have been implemented by the state. Men no longer have the basic right to provide for their families by practicing a profession or a trade. They no longer have a basic right to move from one point to another. These natural rights, which once were taken as a matter of course merely because one was alive, have been destroyed by the state and re-created in the *persona*. One must fulfill state requirements, agree to abide by state rules, submit to state inspection, etc., and then the state will issue a license. The man without the license essentially lacks a *persona*—he has no standing before the state. He can be subject to any kind of treatment without recourse. His business, property, or vehicle can be confiscated. He can be summarily jailed simply because he doesn't have the license/*persona*, not because he has done anything wrong in any absolute sense . . . and so on and so forth.

Likewise, the recent trend to speak of "domestic terrorism" is essentially a move toward dissociating would-be enemies of the state from the broader society and eliminating their *persona* entirely. Whoever is not completely one with the state is a potential enemy. As a potential enemy capable of inflicting almost unlimited damage, he can have no rights, no *persona* before the state. He must be either eliminated or born again within the acceptable parameters of state and society.

The precedents for a rebirth in order to attain personhood in the state are but a shadow of what will happen once a crisis appears. Simply put, anyone who will not submit to having his actions monitored and curtailed as much as the state decides is necessary will be accounted a danger to society and a rebel. If that means submitting to an all-electronic money system, or if it means having a chip implanted under one's skin so his whereabouts can be continuously monitored by satellites, then the *persona* will become conditional on submitting to them. Anyone who refuses to submit to them will be an *unlimited* threat to the state. He is the one who could—who will drop the biotoxin in the water supply. He is worse than a criminal. Worse than a rebel. Having put himself outside the law he is totally at odds with everything and everyone. He must be counted a non-person—somebody who has no rights, and who is a total enemy, deserving only death if he will not repent and be reborn.

While a future in which one's every action is monitored sounds horrible enough, attempts to actually control behavior and so eliminate crime by not allowing it to even be conceived present much more horrible possibilities. An amoral state that considers anything it does to be legitimate, as long as it is done in the name of the people, will certainly explore such possibilities when it is perceived that they are necessary.

Most importantly, all competing loyalties must be eliminated. The two most important competing loyalties in any society are religion and family. Anyone who takes any religious doctrine or writ to be holy can use it to judge the state. It then becomes the basis for taking action against the state. Family goes hand in hand with this, because parents always consider it their responsibility to impart their faith to their children. Even atheistic parents do it, and not always in a way conducive to breeding compliance to state edicts.

Thus, the family must be eliminated. Children must be conceived, brought to viability and then raised by professionals so that they never have parents in any traditional sense. This is already technologically possible. Sperm and egg banks exist and *in vitro* fertilization is now a pretty routine process. Eggs could be implanted in professional foster mothers, etc., etc. The training of such children could be controlled from beginning to end, so that any deviation from the ideal could be dealt with using psychological tools, drugs, etc., or the deviant child could simply be eliminated.

I hesitate to write further of the possibilities, they are so horrible and, honestly, so far out. Yet, briefly ponder the possibilities. Certainly the widespread use of drugs to control human behavior would become routine. Even psycho-surgery, or drug regimens that permanently alter the mind could be put to use where necessary. Human sexuality could be effectively eliminated at the same time that the family is eliminated. Sexual impulses could even be used by the state to train people to be good citizens.[4] Certainly once conception is divorced from intercourse, sexual urges are no longer needed for the preservation of the species in the traditional sense. Scientific breeding could become an important element in control, both for weeding out potentially dangerous genes and encouraging compliance, as well as for breeding men to suit their occupations. After all, a truck driver just doesn't need the intellect necessary to concoct a biological weapon. So a human could be bred for such occupations who simply didn't have that mental capacity, and who would be happy driving trucks all his life. People could be

4 The technology already exists to do this, and professors are writing about it.

conceived and bred exactly according to the needs of society, so there would never be a frustrated scientist who couldn't get a job at a university, and so had to drive a truck instead.

Perhaps worst of all, though, is that free thinking, be it about God, about right and wrong, or anything else will be destroyed as it never has been before. That is the point of all of this. The state will be the all-in-all which defines morals, defines good and evil, right and wrong. It will be the Father and Mother. It will be the Good Shepherd, and it will demand total obedience and, yes, love. The future world that today's state would give us is one in which love is no longer freely ours to give. Rather, it will be cultivated like a desirable physical characteristic in chickens or pigs.

How far will it actually go? Certainly we can say there is no moral principle operating in the modern state to stop it. Whatever is deemed necessary to save the state and save society will be implemented. How much will people put up with? We have had glimpses of just how much people will put up with in history. We have only to look at the Nazis or the communists to see how dark man's heart is. Neither should any of us consider ourselves exempt. Terror can do amazing things to men. If we were at continual risk of being killed, or worse, every moment, and we could not even safely talk to our neighbor for fear of being infected with the latest "mad-cow" disease, few of us would put our rights—or more relevantly, our neighbor's rights—before the simple desire to live. We would want him to have a chip in his head so, if he went berserk and though about going on a shooting spree, he could be stopped.

Secondly, we cannot assume that such miserable principles could not establish a durable state. Although communism has failed, etc., it does not follow that totalitarian control doesn't work. Most of mankind throughout most of history has lived under modern totalitarianism. Liberty is yet a brief experiment. Many now living would apparently think it has not been a worthwhile experiment either.

DO THE SCRIPTURES SPEAK OF SUCH THINGS?

My analysis of where the state is headed has been based on arguments of necessity (in the face of technological development) and moral restraint (or the lack thereof). In other words, the state is headed where it is because it is necessary that it do so in order to survive and because it has no moral scruples about not heading there.

I have intentionally stayed away from the prophetic scriptures because there are so many whacked-out ideas concerning them today. To build another theory on them is to have to defend it against every other theory. To some extent we have to understand that prophecies are veiled—they are not meant to be understood until the time of their fulfillment. Until then, they're going to drive diviners mad.[5] And today's exegetes of the prophetic are little more than diviners in sheep's clothes. These diviners are made mad when they devise theories from scripture and then try to apply them to ever-changing circumstances and new developments. Thus, there have been a steady stream of "prophets" since the days of Christ who have claimed that "now" is the end. Many have set dates for major events, only to watch them come and go. So God makes fools of them. And they deserve it.

On the other hand, one cannot omit to criticize the other extreme as well. To take preterism, the idea that Revelation was fulfilled in the first century, too seriously drives men mad in another way: by annihilating God's effective involvement in modern history. If it was all fulfilled, then God's book is a closed book, and men can expect no more help from Him in working out the coming of His kingdom on earth as it is in heaven. To say that is to drive men mad with despair.

At the same time, when necessity and morality lead us to see such a horrible future, we are inclined to wonder whether God

---

5 Isaiah 44:25

would ever really allow such things. In a way, we've become accustomed to the bizarre and the awful in the fantasy lands of cinema. When we hear and speak of such things, we tend to think of them as fantasies—even if we say we believe them. We don't really put two and two together to see real people, perhaps our own children or grandchildren suffering such miserable fates. It's no more real than the latest video or computer game. Even pop-eschatology turns the horrors into a surreal fantasy by whisking everybody who believes it out before the horrors begin.

In such a climate, invoking the scriptures tends to put the reader into fantasy mode. So I invoke them here only for a very limited purpose. That purpose is to show that God is indeed willing to allow some of the things we've discussed to happen. Obviously some of them have been popularized by modern eschatology. For example, just about every Christian knows about the mark of the beast and the possibility that, at some point in time, men will not be allowed to buy or sell unless they submit to being marked. Such a prophetic vision is not inconsistent with the state's need to monitor financial transactions in order to stop crimes before they are committed.

Not everything we've discussed is well known from the scripture. Modern prophets are, for example, strangely silent about the divorce of sexuality from reproduction. None the less, it can be found in scripture. Daniel appears to refer to it as an important aspect of the latter end of the ten kingdoms in his statement that

> "they shall mingle themselves with the seed of men, but they shall not cleave to one another"—*Daniel 2:43*

Certainly this sounds like the genetic engineering of man and the end of sexual coming together. Yet such expositions of scripture certainly aren't very popular today.

At the same time, we don't see anywhere in scripture a world in which love has been completely destroyed—destroyed to the point where men *can* no longer come to love God. None the less, it might become pretty terrible. Certainly the scriptures speak of a world in which love grows cold—cold enough that men will put one another to death wholesale, and count their abominable works the work of God.

A second reason why I have not turned primarily to scripture to "prove" some kind of future for the modern state is that such proofs tend to confer divine mandates on the future. In other words, if God wills it, who are we to oppose it, and how can it be avoided? So in the end we must just live with it. Or if God has already done it, then why should we expect such possibilities? Both extremes are very dangerous.

My purpose in this book is not to show you that a horror is coming upon the world so we can wring our hands together, but to show ***how to avoid it.*** That is the whole point. At least some of this horror will, in all likelihood, be necessary. Men have become too comfortable in their prosperity and conceit, and only the sting of a whip will dispel this kind of complacency. Likewise, many have bought too deeply into the modern state to let it go, and certainly at least some of them will have to become a special and terrifying example to the rest of the world so that everyone can see where things are headed. Yet, if we know of alternatives and other possibilities in advance of the great crisis, we might indeed short-circuit the worst of the nightmare. Without realistic alternatives, there is no hope.

However far it goes, the future we face at the hands of the state is not pretty. Yet it is coming. It is the future born of a morally bankrupt state and the driving forces of technology which no man can stop. Revolution and the birth of a polity that men can truly believe in is the only alternative.

*

CHAPTER 15

The Sword Unsheathed

The modern Christian lives by the presupposition that he can keep both the laws of God and the laws of the state. Generally, he softens God's laws for this age, even to the point of annulling them, and is careful to keep from running afoul of the state, just for practical reasons. The harlot church is quick to justify the churchman in these presuppositions . . . but are they really adequate?

Given the absolute contention against God at the bottom of man's legal systems, one might suppose that such a positioning is *entirely* inadequate. To the extent that we understand how and where man's laws would drive us to disobey God's laws, it would appear that disobedience to man's law is imperative. Conscience demands it. God commends it as unjust suffering. So what happens when we understand that *every* law of man that differs from God's law is *warring* against God and tearing His law and His kingdom down? Can we avoid the conclusion that we must keep God's law faithfully and reject man's law totally?

> "After the doings of the land of Egypt, where ye dwelt, *shall ye not do,* and after the doings of the land of Canaan, whither I bring you, *shall ye not do,* neither shall ye walk in their ordinances. Ye *shall do* my judgments and keep mine ordinances, to walk therein . . ."—*Leviticus 18:3,4*

In the last analysis there can be no mixing God's law with man's. There is no such thing as a legal system that is "derived from"

God's law. To be *derived* is to be *changed*, and to change God's law is patently *contrary* to God's law,

> "Ye shall not add unto the word which I command you, neither shall ye diminish ought from it, that ye may keep the commandments of the LORD your God which I command you."—*Deuteronomy 4:2*

Changing the law teaches men to change God's law all the more and ignore it. As lawbreaking, it teaches men to break God's law.

This kind of talk all sounds rather theoretical though. What is the man who would please God to do about it? Make a one-man stand against the whole power of the state, only to go down in flames? While one could probably do that without sinning, and become a fine martyr, the chances that it would effect any real change are slim.

For real change to occur, a great falling out must take place. The servants of Jesus Christ must begin to distance themselves from this great monster the state. That distancing does not take the form of rebellion, or court action, or protests and the like. Rather, it involves a simple effort to ***stop sinning*** by individuals. At present, multitudes of people rationalize great sin away because the state makes their sins legal. They haven't given much thought to it because everybody does it and no one thinks about it . . . and of course the harlot never challenges it.

Let me explain . . . .

The scriptures make it plain that God is no respecter of persons.

> "For the LORD your God is God of gods, and Lord of lords, a great God, a mighty, and a terrible, which regardeth not persons, nor taketh reward."—*Deuteronomy 10:17*

> "Wherefore now let the fear of the LORD be upon you, take heed, and do, for there is no iniquity with the LORD our God, no respect of persons."—*2 Chronicles 19:7*

> "For there is no respect of persons with God. For as many as have sinned without law shall also perish without law, and as many as have sinned in the law shall be judged by the law."—*Romans 2:11,12*

> "God accepteth no man's person."—*Galatians 2:6*

> "Your Master also is in heaven, neither is there respect of persons with him"—*Ephesians 6:9*

> "But he that doeth wrong shall receive for the wrong which he hath done, and there is no respect of persons."—*Collosians 3:25*

> "And if ye call on the Father, who without respect of persons judgeth according to every man's work, pass the time of your sojourning here in fear."—*1 Peter 1:17*

Modern Christians tend to look at such statements and understand that the king or president has the same moral accountability to God as ordinary people. He is not exempt. That is true, but the idea that God is no respecter of persons has a much more practical application in this age. Simply put, one's *persona* does not matter to God. Who a man is in society doesn't matter one bit. King or President, citizen or foreigner, legislator or taxpayer, master or slave, all will be judged equally, without regard to the *persona* the state gives them. It doesn't matter what rights or privileges the state has conferred on anyone, great or small. When we stand before the judgement seat of God, there will be no masks, no pretenses to be something, and no excuses. Each will be held strictly accountable to the Word of God, and to God's standards of right and wrong, and only God's standard.

The modern state has created a broad range of rights and privileges for its citizens, and the great multitude drink at this fount regularly. They accept these rights and privileges and revel in them. Herein lies the potential for great sin. If the state demands I surrender my cloak, and I suffer the injustice of this theft and give up my cloak, I do not sin. If it is demanded that I go a mile and I do, there is no sin. Rather, my self-sacrifice and willingness to suffer injustice is counted a virtue before God. On the other hand, if I have the state-granted right to take another's cloak, or to make others go a mile for me, and I use that right to steal from and kidnap men, then I *am* sinning against God. God does not recognize such rights, which are rooted in our *persona*. He does not respect that *persona*, but judges everything righteously according to His law. So if I take someone's cloak, I am a thief in His eyes. If I force him to go with me I am a kidnaper, whether the state gives me that privilege or not.

The modern state steals money from people and gives it to others with more political clout. Each *persona* is legally entitled to some form of grant from the Great Provider, the state. To knowingly take stolen goods, that have been confiscated under the color of laws passed at *your* behest by politicians *you* put in office with *your* votes is no different than going out with a gun and putting it to someone's head and demanding their wallet. God doesn't recognize the laws you use to justify yourself. He doesn't recognize your state-granted right to take what belongs to another.

In reality, such "benefits" are not merely theft. They also constitute accepting a bribe. A bribe, or gift, blinds the eyes and turns back truth and justice.

> "And thou shalt take no gift, for the gift blindeth the wise, and perverteth the words of the righteous."—*Exodus 23:8*

These bribes, paid to millions and promised to millions more, cause people to turn a blind eye to the injustice of the theft involved and wink at the ungodly state. They prefer an ungodly state and will resist the truth of God's word concerning the state. In the end, they are paid servants of a state that is in total rebellion to God. They are therefore themselves rebels against God who have no share in Him. If they claim to be Christians, they are either totally ignorant of the truth or they are impostors, pure and simple. They deny God's law and support the state for pay—harlots.

Now, dear reader, I realize that you may be among those who are taking bribes and blood money from the state. Most people are, in one form or another. Now that you understand the truth, you're going to have to make a decision. That decision may be painful in the extreme. It may require faith you don't believe you have. *Your eternal salvation is at stake though.* You now understand the law. You understand your standing at the last judgement, and that man's law won't come into play there. Like the Nazis at Nuremburg, your defense of just obeying the law or obeying orders won't have any standing. If you reject the truth you understand, you prove yourself a rebel and no friend of Christ. Ignorance may have shielded you in the past, but it can no longer.

> "And the times of this ignorance God winked at, but now commandeth all men every where to repent."—*Acts 17:30*

God does not smile stupidly upon those who willfully choose to continue in sin after coming to a knowledge of the truth. "He that doeth wrong shall receive for the wrong which he hath done, and there is no respect of persons." That is the *New* Testament. The *only* salvation is to repent and turn from this horrid evil. Unless and until you do, you are a paid minion of the devil, and working to maintain man's ancient rebellion against God. God is not like you. He does not accept rewards and bribes. Your lot is hell. You cannot serve God and mammon. You've loved mammon and hated God. If that is not true, then why do you take stolen goods and vote for politicians that steal? You support the state, and it supports you. That is the root and foundation of modern politics. It's why a rebellious, ungodly state stays in power, even though a majority claim to be Christians.

You've got to come out and be separate. You've got to cut off all the government aid, social security, welfare, unemployment, publicly funded schools and day care, subsidized medical care and drugs, subsidized housing, subsidized food, school loans, housing loans, business loans . . . all of it. Stop making excuses saying "oh, I've paid in, so I can take a little". If your neighbor on your right comes and robs you, does that entitle you to go rob your neighbor on the left to make up for it? Two wrongs do not make a right. *All of it has to go.* You're better off getting rid of your house, closing your business, etc. Yes, you're better off standing on the street corner begging than willfully sinning after you know the truth. Even if you get pneumonia from standing out in the rain and and die early, it's better to die sooner and go to heaven than to live long and well and end up in hell. If you reject this, it only proves that

You don't believe God's word.
You are a hypocrite, a lie and a lover of lies.
You hate the truth.
You are indeed a thief.
You are a paid minion of rebels against God.
You are a servant of Satan.

The times of ignorance are at an end. *Now. Today.* How can you claim to love your neighbor when your hired agent, the state, is holding a gun to his head, robbing him for you? You've redefined love, not according to God's standards, but according to your own. You smile and say "hello" while the Revenue Service agents are taking his home and putting him out on the street, and you say you love him! That's *your* hypocritical standard. But if you steal from him, God will say *you never loved him at all.* You didn't just refuse him a drink when he was thirsty. You didn't just walk by him on the road when he had been waylaid. You helped to waylay him! That's God's standard.

"And this is love, that we walk after his commandments."—*2 John 6*

If you cannot stand free from condemnation in this, then repent, and forswear such tainted money. God will forgive you and open His arms to you.

A godly revolution can never happen if the revolutionaries are hypocrites. They have to be true believers. It can never happen when those who claim to be faithful are really Judases, paid spies and traitors to the enemy.

THE BEGINNING OF REVOLUTION

Very well. You now understand what price must be paid to be a revolutionary. Yet this is only the price that must be paid to be a Christian. In the end, whose laws you obey determines who is Lord of your life. If you accept man's definitions of right and wrong, and use them to nullify God's definitions, then He cannot be your Lord. Man makes this the easiest thing in the world to do. The true Christian must resist.

Everyone who claims to serve Jesus Christ must be brought to a point of decision. The truth about God's law and man's must be spread abroad despite the harlot church's opposition to it, and Christians must be brought to a place where they will decide whom they will serve. This isn't merely a polite matter of converting some people or creating a new sect on the basis of some new doctrine. It's basic morality that transcends denominational lines on the one hand, and total division on the other. Those who continue taking stolen money after they know the truth are declaring in no uncertain terms that they are *not* going to serve Christ and that they are quite happy to have you be their milk cow. They will use the force of the state to rob you and your children, *no matter what anyone thinks about it* (including God). There will be no fellowship between such sons of hell and the children of light. How can there be? Christ came to make us free indeed, and not into the milk cows of the unrighteous. Those who refuse the truth will hate the truth speakers as long as they speak the truth. They will reject them and cast them out because they will not be able to abide the truth clearly spoken. Thus will come the basic moral division essential for revolution to take place.

Understand that what I am saying here is not merely straining at a gnat. If Christ could say that merely to look at a woman lustfully is to be an adulterer, that merely to hate your brother is to be a murderer, then would it not be appropriate to say that merely to cast a covetous eye upon your neighbor's goods is to be a thief? How much more, then, if you actually take those goods under the color of law!

Neither are these bribes bestowed by the state a small matter. It is of strategic importance in the cosmic battle between heaven and hell. The modern state has a tremendous legitimacy problem—a problem that is practically growing day by day. So the state buys people off and keeps them from questioning its legitimacy with bribes—bribes paid with stolen money. Spiritually speaking, sin puts people in bondage. Bribes blind them.

They cannot get free. They come to have a slave mentality and don't want to get free. Take these bribes out of the way and the very legitimacy of the state will become a central issue.

Likewise, God's judgement will be unleashed against those who know the truth and reject it. Their very sins will be their undoing. When all the potential horrors of the modern state begin to be unleashed against its subjects, these who reject the truth will have nowhere else to turn, and will become slaves such as the world has never seen or known.

Those who accept the truth, though, will have their eyes opened. They're no longer blinded by bribes. They'll be able to see right and walk clearly. They won't be paid servants of the state. It will no longer have anything in them. These can begin to work for righteousness with an undivided heart. They can reason out further consequences of the great contention between man's law and God's law.

If a few people will but understand the contention between man's law and God's law, and choose to serve God and not man to the extent that they will deny their own *persona* and refuse a bribe from the thief-state then the revolution has begun. From this point, it must grow in breadth and depth.

Christians do not press the claims of God's law against this world because they themselves are unwilling to live by it. They generally prefer their own laws. That's why those laws exist in the first place—people voted them into place. However, those who come out from dependency upon the state gain independence from it. The blindness caused by the bribe begins to lift, and they can begin to reason clearly.

As people are willing to accept the claim of God's law in one area, and declare the state's laws immoral, refusing a benefit the law confers, then a wedge has been driven into the moral principle of the state. If one group of laws is immoral, then what about others? And what can be done about it?

The Christian revolutionary must pursue a moral revolution—a revolution with a moral end, carried out by moral means. Yet by "moral" we mean not the foul, false morality of the state, which supports the state and puts God down. Herein lies the revolutionary prerogative. Those who keep God's law and do not sin against it *do not sin at all.* They are not in danger of hell fire. In particular, the state does not have the power to open and close heaven with its laws, any more than the pope had such power in the old times. Liberated from such a power, the revolutionary is holden only to God's law. Specifically, he can morally break the state's laws, so long as he does not break God's law. Once the nature of the contention between the two legal systems is understood, any such civil disobedience becomes a matter of conscience, because all of man's laws put down God's laws. Once the righteous have gained independence from the state's laws by shunning their benefits, they can righteously judge those laws, and press the claims of God's law against the state.

Such claims can—and indeed must—be pressed against the state in two distinct ways. First, they must be pressed in terms of the Christian's basic right to live by God's law. The state has no business punishing men for what is not sin—what is not wrong. Furthermore, it has no business punishing men except on God's command, and as God commands they be punished. A Christian has a right to be free from bondage to the arbitrary law of men.

Second, when the state attempts to so enslave men, it positively violates God's law. The claims of God's law must be pressed against the state and its officials, even as they press their own claims to legitimacy against the revolution. Such officials hide behind their *persona*, but they must be stripped of that *persona* and judged by God's law, without respect to persons.

Such claims are more than enough to push a revolution through to completion. On the one hand they can be asserted to free the godly man who would live by God's laws from his bondage to the ungodly state. On the other hand, they can be asserted to punish the minions of the state who violate God's law under the pretense of their own law.

Thus, for example, the godly need not, in any absolute sense, abide by all the multitude of inane regulations which the state creates. They do not owe taxes. They do not have to obey everything from environmental regulations to speed limits to zoning regulations. When taxes are levied, or unlawful fines imposed, those who impose and collect them *can* lawfully be treated as what they are in God's eyes—thieves and robbers. When men are unjustly imprisoned their captors can be treated as what they are, kidnapers. In this manner, the modern state can be systematically disempowered as the alternative gains momentum.

Of course, there is a great need for wisdom in such a revolutionary program. The strength of the modern state is formidable. Obviously, it has already crushed many individuals who have stood up to its ungodly laws on the basis of principle, and it will continue to do so. Likewise, it will continue to crush any group that rises against it, so long as it is able to do so.

On the other hand, the technology-driven power shift we are facing could put even a small group of revolutionaries in a position where they could literally destroy a large nation and virtually everyone in it. This is a sobering possibility. Faced with it, we must take to heart Jesus' admonition that "he who lives by the sword dies by the sword." Even if we could obliterate this or that government, is that what we should seek? Indeed, if we do, what is to keep the next guy from obliterating us?

In the end, we have to make a break from traditional ideas of statecraft. The point of a revolution is not to force our will on all of mankind or all of the people in a particular territory. The point is not to make every atheist or Hindu knuckle under. The point is to establish a godly government for people who want it and truly believe in it. The point is not to create a world government or super-state that reaches from sea to shining sea. The point is to create a Christian community. That may mean a few hundred people or a federation that covers hundreds of square miles. Those who don't believe and don't want it can live in a different community.

The way to get such a government is not by destroying the old, but by separating from it. Those who want a welfare state, and who want to keep their checks coming in can do that. Why should anyone care to stop them? They can have hell on earth with it, too, if they want to. What really concerns us is not what they do, *but that they don't drag us along with them*, and force us to sin with them, to stain our hands with the blood of the saints, and to live in their hell.

Obviously, the modern state, which is all based on coercion instead of true faith, will not want to lose its milk cows. As such, it is pointless to talk about revolution unless there is the threat of force behind it. The only language evil men understand is force. Should we shrink back from that language, so long as we are careful to use ***just*** force (just according to God's true word) and to use it wisely? Can we use it justly and wisely? Such questions are so context sensitive that it is perhaps pointless to even discuss them from the comfort of our armchairs. They can only honestly be breached in real life situations and circumstances. After all, if men simply rise up against a state that is not bothering them, it is a far different matter than if they rise up in response to a state that has just ordered them to report to the nearest government clinic for body modification and chip implantation.

We must realize that it is not realistic to use any kind of force against the state until it is really and truly breaking down. In such a context one is not merely discussing the use of force against a united state that in unquestionably in control. It becomes more a matter of using force to establish a government where there really isn't an effective government anymore, where perhaps various factions, rogues, gangs, militias and invaders are vying for control. Given the fact that small groups are gaining the power to seriously challenge the state, such a scenario is no longer merely some pie-in-the-sky dream for generations to come. We are very likely to see it within the next ten years.

Likewise, if used wisely and circumspectly by those who understand the ramifications, it may be that not very much force will have to actually be used. If one could simply *demonstrate* to a renegade state or pseudo-state that one has the capacity to destroy it without question, it is conceivable that a bloodless secession could be accomplished.

In any event, it must be recognized that the use of force may be entirely appropriate in certain situations . . . and those situations are made all the more clear by properly understanding God's laws as they apply to the state. So the key for today is not to seek an immediate direct confrontation with the state, but to wage a war of ideas to weaken the consensus behind it by drawing individuals away from it. At the same time, believers have to reason out their faith and begin to live, as it were, in the new Christian community now. They have to stop taking bribes. Many will have to change their professions and find new livelihoods. We will have to establish a system of godly justice among us. We will have to help the aged who join us, for it is not right to call them out of the world system and then throw them out on the street. And so on and so forth. In short, there is no waiting until after a successful revolution to build a new government a new community and a new world. The revolution becomes real as we establish a revolutionary Christian community and a revolutionary government here and now. Then, as revolutionary principles and consistent biblical morals combine with the already failing legitimacy of the state and the technological empowerment of small groups, the fall of the modern state may prove closer than anyone could hope to think.

*

CHAPTER 16
Another Future

As the sword of truth divides the church and weeds out the true believers from the pretenders, it will also be a standard to draw men to it. When faced with the realities of what the modern state is becoming and the prospect of having to become part of it, many people who would today ignore both the scriptures and any idea of a biblical government will have good reason to reconsider.

The extremely limited government that a consistent biblical understanding of law engenders acts to establish a great deal of freedom on a very solid foundation. Simply put, whatever God's law doesn't forbid is permitted to the individual. Where the community has no sanction from God to impose a penalty, it cannot. Where it has no authority to act, it must refrain. Thus, in a biblical society the community government would own no property, collect no taxes, and have no employees. It would not license or regulate anything, and it would not provide the vast array of services which the modern state does. These would all be left in private hands. In the end, the individual would simply be free to live his own life. Hopefully when he did that he would read the Bible and try to conform his life to what the Bible teaches—yet even in that, there is no community dictate to force him to. And much of the scriptures are, in the end, left to private interpretation.

This paradigm of government—the biblical paradigm—cannot really wear a modern label of conservative or liberal. It comes from a different mold altogether. In truth, it would allow some surprising things. For example, it would be perfectly legal to smoke a marijuana cigarette in public. The scriptures nowhere condemn that, per se. They do caution against drunkenness, but it is up to the individual, not the community to decide if that even applies to marijuana, and to decide how much is too much. Likewise, the scriptures admonish a woman to dress modestly (1 Timothy 2:9), but it is up to the individual to decide what that means. Is it talking about a short skirt here, or about wearing costly jewelry that drains a family's budget so it cannot do good works? In the end, there is no community law about clothing at all. So it would be perfectly legal to walk down the street naked.[1] It would be perfectly legal to walk down the street cross dressed.[2] It isn't the community government's place to try to make men sinless with legislation. After all, it isn't many laws that bring men to love God. In a biblical society, the community government and the community's judges could only set an example of proper behavior by respecting peoples' freedom. To expand on God's law is sin, so for the community government to expand on the charger God has given it and intrude into men's freedoms is to sin. Yet, to willfully sin is to rationalize sin away, and as soon as this government rationalizes sin away in itself, it destroys its own foundation.

In the end, if the revolution is true to God's word, and avoids becoming the mistress of modern political and religious conservatives, it could have a broad appeal among many people who care little for the things of God at present. The church has followed the state in making man's word the standard of right and wrong in many ways. It has changed God's standards because it prefers an outward beauty and respectability to true righteousness. So it rejects someone who lives in a shack and has

---

1 Two Old Testament prophets apparently did as much. See Isaiah 20:3 and Micah 1:8

2 Even though the scriptures condemn it as an abomination (Deut 22:5), no punishment is specified for it. As such, it is up to the individual to keep this law. Practically there is a reason for this: Drawing the lines where cross dressing starts is not always cut and dried. For example, is a man wearing earrings violating Deut 22:5? Is a woman wearing slacks? And so on. Much of it depends on styles, and styles certainly do change with time.

only nasty clothes to wear to church, and it rejects the person who likes wearing a nose ring, but it accepts thieves among its numbers and affords them places of honor.

So to return to the Bible and draw a true line between right and wrong is nothing different than what Jesus did, rightly dividing the word of God and extending grace to unlovely and lowly people who could come and learn the truth without first having to measure up to the false pharisaical standard of righteousness. Like the servant who could not get the invited guests to come to the marriage feast, and so went out into the streets to get people who would come, many churchmen will not have God's laws or godly government. So if a godly revolution is finally peopled with those who have rarely been inside a church, it should be no surprise.

Even so, it is not reasonable to expect that a specifically Christian revolution or government is going to somehow take over the world, or even a single major nation today. There is simply too much anti-christian sentiment. There are too many people who would rather die than submit to a "christian theocracy" or whatever they might call it. Likewise, there are too many people who really do serve mammon, and who really do prefer to keep getting the government checks, even if it means going to hell over it, or having hell come up on the earth to take them. So how could a godly revolution possibly succeed?

First it is necessary to understand that it has never been God's desire to somehow force men to serve Him. He gave Adam and Eve a certain freedom of will that they chose to exercise wrongly. Likewise, He has never, from the beginning, forced His government on people. That is not to say that people have not paid a terrible price for bad government, because we all reap what we sow, but that He doesn't force us to do this or that. Even ancient Israel agreed to receive the government God gave them (Deuteronomy 27) and it lasted only until they decided they wanted a king instead (1 Samuel 8). Neither is it any different today. The point is not to force the ungodly to live like Christians, but to force them to stop forcing real Christians to live like the ungodly. The point is not to "beat" existing governments, but to gain the freedom to separate ways and depart from them. No die hard atheist, no Moslem need ever be forced into submitting to a Christian government. By the same token, no Christian should ever be forced to submit to a Moslem government or an atheistic representative republic. And if Egypt won't let God's people go to serve Him truly, then Egypt deserves to be judged and destroyed.

Any government must be founded on some absolute authority, on some word or some idea that is beyond questioning. What that absolute should be will be debated among men. Some will say it should be the voice of the people and the vote, others the voice of the King, the Pope, or the Elite. Some will say it should be the writings of Marx and Lennin. Some will say it should be the Bible, others the Koran, etc. Yet this absolute must exist. It is unavoidable.

Much of human history has merely been a history of men trying to forcefully impose their absolutes on others. The problem is that brute force can never successfully repress the truth or advance the truth. People never really change their beliefs because someone holds a gun to their heads. They might do so outwardly, but inwardly they will seethe with resentment and in their hearts they can only work to undermine the beliefs they're forced to accept. Much of the antipathy against Christianity in the modern world is simply due to the fact that Christian morals are the traditional basis for the laws of modern republics, and modern republics attempt to force people of many varied beliefs to live together under one law and one moral system.

The modern republics were an attempt to solve this problem of absolutes by doing away with a religious absolute. They did succeed in a sense. They short-circuited the persecution of earlier ages. No longer would people die because they wouldn't declare fealty to the Pope, or because they would not attend an official government church. Yet the problem of absolutes came back to haunt the republic because absolutes ultimately determine how men will live. Different absolutes lead to different determinations of good and evil, and different laws. Ultimately, because the republic does not succeed at getting beyond absolutes and does not leave men free to work out their absolutes in real life, it must become every bit as terrible and insane as a church that burned men alive if they read the Bible.

In the end, man's desire to unite the whole world under one kind of government and one absolute, be it by force or by wise engineering of the government involved, must fail. The answer cannot be found by setting up one absolute and forcing all men to kowtow to it. Rather, the answer is in a multiplicity of absolutes, and a multiplicity of governments to go with them. Freedom of religion does not consist of mixing all different people together and saying they're free to believe what they wish privately, as long as they submit to the laws of the state. It consists of allowing people to physically separate and develop their own ideas and their own laws.

Thus, one must not think of the post-revolutionary world as one gigantic Christian New World Order. Rather, imagine a patchwork quilt of communities, some large, some small, with all variety of beliefs. Some are Christian. Some are atheists and anarchists. Some are Islamic kingdoms. Some orthodox Jewish theocracies. Some are representative republics. Each works out its own laws and destiny.

Realistically, only such a patchwork quilt of little, locally controlled countries, each consisting of true believers in whatever the principles of those countries are—only this kind of arrangement will ever accommodate the technological realities of the future. Only such an arrangement can contain the possibility of one man having the power to destroy a whole nation, without having to resort to unlimited tyranny. Rather than containing him through force, he can be restrained by true faith. Simply put, why destroy a government that you believe—truly believe—is the best possible and is essentially right? And if you don't believe it is right, you can take your pick of other countries to go to—perhaps tens of thousands of them—places that really are different and offer real possibilities for living very differently. At the same time these small countries could live at peace because each one would potentially be more powerful than the most powerful nation on earth today. So it would be futile to fight for territory, etc. This kind of a vision for the future is something that could attract people from a wide variety of backgrounds and beliefs . . . certainly enough people to give a revolution the momentum it needed to succeed. It is the only sane solution for what the world is coming to. The only people it doesn't cater to are the megalomaniacs who want to keep everybody under their thumb. These megalomaniacs think God is like them—a God whose return means bloody war, and the violent destruction of all His enemies through brute force. They've taught untolled millions to believe the same thing.

Yet what about the fact that during the millennium there will be other nations (Revelation 20:8)? The millennium could be something very different from what most people imagine. Micah is even more specific in his vision of this millennium:

> [1]But in the last days it shall come to pass, that the mountain of the house of the LORD shall be established in the top of the mountains, and it shall be exalted above the hills, and the people shall flow unto it.
> [2]And many nations shall come, and say, "Come, and let us go up to the mountain of the LORD, and to the house of the God of Jacob, and he will teach us of his ways, and we will walk in his paths," for the law shall go forth of Zion, and the word of the LORD from Jerusalem. [3]And he shall judge among many people, and rebuke strong nations afar off, and they shall beat their swords into plowshares, and their spears into pruninghooks: nation shall not lift up a sword against nation, neither shall they learn war any more. [4]But they shall sit every man under his vine and under his fig tree, and none shall make them afraid, for the mouth of the LORD of hosts hath spoken it. [5]For all people will walk every one in the name of his god, and we will walk in the name of the LORD our God for ever and ever. [6]In that day, saith the LORD, will I assemble her that halteth, and I will gather her that is driven out, and her that I have afflicted. [7]And I will make her that halted a remnant, and her that was cast far off a strong nation, and the LORD shall reign over them in mount Zion henceforth, even for ever.—*Micah 4:1-7*

This is an incredible passage. It speaks of the last days, the establishment of God's kingdom, the restoration of God's law, the establishment of peace and the reassembly and healing of the dispersed people of God. Yet right in the middle of it—verse five—it says "For all people will walk every one in the name of his god, and we will walk in the name of Yahweh our God". This is not speaking of a world in which everyone serves only Yahweh. Rather, it is speaking of a world in which men serve different gods, but in which they do not attempt to force others to mouth things that they do not truly believe.

In such a world, the truth can compete freely against the lies, and Christ can slay those who believe the lies ***with the sword of truth.*** As false religions and ideas become at once free to work out the logical consequences of their beliefs and impotent to blame their failures on scapegoats, every god will be fully revealed for what it is. And when revealed for the unclean things they are, false gods will be abandoned and the mountain of the LORD will be exalted.

So in the end, the answer for mankind in the coming millennium is not techno-tyranny, but an answer similar to that adopted by a small group of pilgrims hundreds of years ago as their ship lay off the coast of a great wilderness. Realizing they would soon land in a place where no human government existed, they came together and voluntarily covenanted to live by the laws of their God according to their faith, and so formed the first government indigenous to the new world, leaving behind the old world of governments which held men captive from birth, and which exerted a tyranny over their very thoughts and beliefs.

There is another future we can have if we are willing to pay the price for it. If, like those pilgrims of old, we are willing to break our ties with the past and lift up our eyes and look to a better future and a better country, however far off the shores of that better country may be, then God will bless us and lead us to those shores and to a life where we can truly live our faith without hindrance.

***

An Afterword

I realize that in these pages I have called some people out of a bondage to sin and the state which is going to take some serious effort to get free from. You may see that you are one of them. You need to do that, but you don't know how. Some of the pits we've dug for ourselves are pretty deep.

First and foremost, make a commitment today that you will get free, whatever it takes. You may not know how, you may not even think it possible. Don't look at the difficulty of the task and determine your morality (or lack of it) on that basis, though. Look to God. If the Holy Spirit has convicted you, and God's word has convicted you, then God will make a way if you set your heart to obey. The first step is to make a decision to go out. Next, seek Him in prayer for answers. Above all, don't fall into the trap of saying "I can't". Of course you can't . . . but God can. And He will, too.

At the same time, I realize that to say "be warm and be filled" and yet fail to lift a finger to help those who need it would be sin on my part. So if you need help seeing your way out of this bondage, I will do what I can for you. Write to me in care of the publisher, Lexington & Concord Partners, and tell me your situation. I will pray for you, give you ideas, advice, direction, etc. If you truly need it, I'll even help you find support through people who are voluntarily willing to give it, so you can stop being a thief and be free from bondage and blindness.

The first step is that decision to get free and get out of the system. Really, it's critical, not only from the standpoint of pleasing God, but also, it's critical to avoid being sucked into the techno-tyranny that is fast approaching. Those who have become dependent on the state are the very ones who will be the foundation for this tyranny. The state will justify doing anything it deems necessary to continue its existence because of all of these "poor people" who are dependent on it. Their lives have become dependent on forcing others to submit to being robbed. Such as these will be the curse and byword of generations to come.

Appendix A

A Sample Legal Code

The following is a straightforward codification of God's law for a Christian community. These laws are discussed in detail in the companion volume to this book, *True Christian Government*, available from the publishers.

The Community Law

This code is intended as an aid to understanding the laws of God which are delegated to the community to enforce. It does not have higher authority than the scriptures themselves. Neither is it a complete statement of all of God's laws which an individual is responsible to God to obey.

I. Worship of the true god Yahweh

1. Anyone found sacrificing to any god but Yahweh shall be put to death. (Ex 22:20)

2. Anyone sacrificing a child shall be stoned to death. (Lev 20:2, Deut 18:10)

3. Anyone enticing others to worship or serve any god but Yahweh shall be stoned to death, a prophetic utterance which comes to pass notwithstanding (Deut 13:6-10, Deut 13:1-5).

4. Anyone who having been a believer turns away from the true God and Jesus Christ his son to serve other gods, false religions, or created things shall be stoned to death. (Deut 17:2-5)

5. If a group of people including a whole town or city shall violate Section I.4, all offenders shall be afforded the same

punishment, even if civil war is necessary. In the event of war, the offenders shall be totally destroyed. (Deut 13:12-16)

6. Witches, wizards, diviners, enchanters, necromancers and consulters with familiar spirits shall be stoned to death. (Ex 22:18, Lev 20:27, Deut 18:10)

a) The above mentioned are understood to be using spells, incantations, supernatural power, etc., for their gain, and not merely victims thereof.

b) Victims of inhabiting spirits, curses, etc., shall be delivered by the power of Jesus Christ.

c) Demonic possession shall not be a defense against crimes committed under such influence.

7. Anyone who speaks prophetically in the name of Yahweh and his word does not come to pass shall be put to death. (Deut 18:20-22)

8. Anyone blaspheming Yahweh, either by libel or by claiming to be God, shall be put to death. (Lev 24:16)

9. For the purposes of I.3, I.4 and I.5, a false religion and false god shall be understood as any which does not acknowledge Yahweh to be the only God and creator of the universe, and Jesus Christ as his only begotten son come in the flesh, and the 66 books of the Bible as inspired of God, worshiping God and Jesus Christ as such. (1 John 4:1,2, 1 John 2:23)

10. Each family shall choose one day in the week as a sabbath. Employers who refuse to respect this day and allow employees that day off shall be put to death. (Ex 31:13-16)

11. At the beginning of every seventh year AD, all debts are annulled and common servants are declared free. (Deut 15:1,2)

12. On the tenth day of the seventh month of every forty ninth year AD, title to all land, except that owned in areas originally designated within the boundary of a city, shall revert to the family which originally owned it (Lev 25:23-28), and all slaves except foreign bondslaves and those who have chosen to be permanent slaves of their own free will are free. (Lev 25:39-57) (See V.7)

II. Marriage and Sexual Relationships

1. If any man or woman has any form of sexual intercourse with a beast, both the person and the beast shall be put to death. (Ex 22:19, Lev 20:15,16)

2. If a man has any form of sexual intercourse with another man, both shall be put to death. (Lev 20:13)

3. If a man has any form of sexual intercourse with his father's wife, both shall be put to death (Lev 20:11)

4. If a man has any form of sexual intercourse with his daughter in law, both shall be put to death. (Lev 20:12)

5. If a man has any form of sexual intercourse with a woman and her mother, all three shall be burned to death (Lev 20:14)

6. If a man has any form of sexual intercourse with a married or betrothed woman, both shall be put to death. (Lev 20:10, Deut 22:22-27)

7. For the purposes of II.3, II.4, II.5, and II.6, the woman or women involved will be adjudged not guilty if they claim to have screamed, and could not have been heard screaming, or were heard and no one responded to the screams. In such a case the man will be put to death and the woman will go free.

8. A man having any kind of sexual intercourse with a virgin shall: (Deut 22:28,29, Ex 22:16,17)

a) Pay the woman's father fifty shekels of silver.

b) Take the woman to be his wife, unless the father refuses.

c) He may not divorce her.

9. A man may divorce his wife if he finds uncleanness in her, by giving her a written bill of divorce. (Deut 24:1-4)

10. A woman suspected of adultery may be brought to the judges by her husband. The judges will pray over her, and ask her to receive a curse if the accusation be true. The judgement of God will then be accepted by all. (Num 5:12-31)

11. The daughter of any believing father in the community who commits harlotry shall be burned to death. (Lev 21:9, 1 Pet 2:9)

III. Parent and child

1. Whoever curses their father or mother shall be put to death. (Ex 21:17)

2. Whoever smites his father or mother shall be put to death. (Ex 21:15)

3. If father and mother request of the judges that a rebellious son be put to death, their request shall be carried out. (Deut 21:18-21)

IV. Murder

1. The refuge cities shall be ______, ______ and ______.

2. Anyone who kills a person may have refuge against the revenger of blood in a refuge city designated in Section IV.1 until they can be tried. (Num 35:11-33)

3. The person found by the judges to have committed willful murder shall be given over to the avenger of blood. (Deut 19:11-13)

a) The use of a weapon of war in the killing implies an intentional killing. (Num 35:16)

b) In the event there is no avenger of blood, the murderer shall in any event be put to death. (Lev 24:17)

4. The person found to have killed someone accidentally may have sanctuary in the refuge city against the revenger of blood.

a) If the revenger so desires, he may take the life of the killer if he is found outside the refuge city before the death of the chief judge holding office when the case was tried. (Num 35:26-28)

b) After the death of the chief judge, the killer will be free to return to his home.

c) Only the avenger of blood may forgive a killer and choose not to take revenge on him if he returns to his home at any specified time before the death of the chief judge. (Num 35:32)

5. The judges of the nearest town to the scene of a murder shall diligently investigate the murder if the murderer is not found, and pray that God would forgive them for the blood so shed. (Deut 21:1-9)

6. If an animal kills a man it shall be stoned to death, (Ex 21:28-32)

a) If the animal was known to be dangerous, the owner shall also be put to death

b) The avenger of blood may lay a price on the owner instead of seeking his life.

c) The price for a servant or slave shall be thirty shekels of silver. The price for other persons shall be negotiable.

V. Violence

1. Any person who wounds another, accidentally or intentionally, shall pay for the wounded person to be thoroughly healed, and pay for his loss of time. (Ex 21:18,19)

2. If anyone causes a blemish in another, as he has done, so shall it be done unto him, breach for breach, eye for eye, tooth for tooth. (Lev 24:19,20)

3. A woman who takes a man by the private parts in a fight shall have her hand cut off. (Deut 25:11,12)

4. Whoever kidnaps anyone shall be put to death. (Ex 21:16, Deut 24:7)

5. The unborn child is a person. If a woman carrying a child is injured so that she delivers the child, (Ex 21:22-25)

a) If the child is not otherwise injured, the judges shall lay a fine upon the person causing the premature birth.

b) If the child is injured, Sections V.1, V.2 and Section IV apply.

VI. Property

1. Concerning theft and robbery,

a) Anyone caught in the act of stealing something may be pursued and killed until the sun rises again. (Ex 22:1-4)

b) Anyone voluntarily confessing a theft must restore it, plus a fifth of its value to the person it was stolen from. (Lev 6:2-5)

c) Anyone who stole anything who is caught with it must restore double. (Ex 22:4)

d) Anyone who stole something and sold, killed or destroyed it must pay for it four times over if valued at 20 shekels of silver or less, and five times over if valued over 20 shekels of silver. (Ex 22:1-3)

2. Anyone who owes money or goods as a result of a theft he committed and a court decision against him and cannot pay it shall be sold as a slave for the debt. (Ex 22:1-4)

3. If someone is keeping anything in trust for someone, and a controversy arises due to loss, or because both claim it to be theirs, (Ex 22:7-15)

a) If it was stolen, and the thief is found, he shall repay double.

b) If stolen and the thief is not found, killed by wild animals, or otherwise taken or driven away, the keeper shall take an oath that he has not put his hand to his neighbor's goods, and he shall not make it good.

c) If the keeper has taken of the goods, he shall repay double.

d) If the person claiming the goods of the keeper doesn't own them, he shall pay the keeper double

4. If a man borrows something from his neighbor and it is hurt, damaged or killed, he shall pay for it. (Ex 22:14,15)

a) If the owner hired the animal or thing out, the man using it shall not pay for it.

b) If the owner was present with the animal or thing, it is assumed it was hired out.

5. Anyone who causes another's property to be damaged, destroyed or killed shall cause it to be restored. (Ex 22:5,6, Lev 24:18, 21)

6. If a man opens a pit and his neighbor's animal shall fall into it and die, the animal shall be his, and he shall pay his neighbor for it. (Ex 21:33,34)

7. If two neighbors' animals fight and one kills the other, then: (Ex 21:35,36)

a) The live one shall be sold and the money and the dead animal shall be divided between them.

b) If the live animal be known to have pushed or gored in the past, then the owner of the dead animal shall get the live one, and the dead one will go to the owner of the live one.

8. On the tenth day of the seventh month of every forty ninth year AD, title to all land, except that owned in areas originally designated within the boundary of a city, shall revert to the family which originally owned it (Lev 25:23-28), and all slaves except foreign bondslaves and those who have chosen to be permanent slaves of their own free will are free. (Lev 25:39-57) (See I.12)

VII. Slavery

1. A man can sell his son or daughter as a servant.

a) A son is to serve until the beginning of the next sabbath year, except he be redeemed by his family for the price paid for him, prorated to the time of his release. (Ex 21:2-4)

b) A daughter shall be assumed to be betrothed to the man who bought her, his son, or his male servant. She may be kept by her master, or redeemed by her father or her father's family at the price paid for her and returned to her father's house. (Ex 21:7-11)

2. A man may be sold for his debts.

a) In such a case, he shall serve until the beginning of the jubilee. (Lev 25:47-49)

b) He may be redeemed by his family for the amount of his original purchase price less the proportion of time he has served. (Lev 25:50-52)

3. Foreigners who are not Christians when acquired may be kept as permanent, hereditary bondslaves. (Lev 25:44-46)

a) Such slaves may be freed only if unowned land is available and they obtain a parcel through the proper channels.

4. A servant may willingly choose to permanently remain the slave of his master. (Ex 21:5-7) In such a case,

a) His decision shall be announced by himself before a judge of the community

b) His ear shall be pierced

c) He shall serve his master for ever.

5. A servant shall receive his freedom, if he or she desires it, (Ex 21:26,27)

a) For loss of an eye

b) For loss of a tooth

6. If a master beats a slave so that he dies within 24 hours, he shall be guilty of murder, but not if the slave lives longer than 24 hours. (Ex 21:20,21)

7. A servant who has escaped from his master should not be returned to that master, unless he was sold for debt incurred as a result of crime (Deut 23:15,16).

VIII. The courts and the judiciary

1. A judge which accepts a gift or bribe which might affect his judgement is dismissed from office on the date of receipt of the gift and forbidden to hold office in the future. Any judgement which might have been affected by the gift shall be reviewed by a higher judge. (Deut 16:19,20)

2. All cases presented to a judge shall be heard within seven days of presentation, unless mutually agreed by both parties involved. (Ex 18:22,26)

3. No one shall be condemned or punished except at least two, or at the discretion of the judge, three witnesses can testify against the defendant. (Deut 17:6,7, Deut 19:15)

4. A false witness who testifies falsely against anyone shall be punished with the punishment which he sought to have inflicted on the person he testified against. (Deut 19:16-19)

5. Anyone who refuses to obey a judge's order in a case presented to that judge shall be put to death. (Deut 17:12)

6. A judge may order anyone appearing before his court to be beaten with up to forty strokes for wickedness of any kind related to the trial. (Deut 25:1-3)

7. A case may be sent to a higher court if the judges hearing it cannot decide the matter, being at odds with one another, or wish to send it to a higher court.

Index

Scripture Index

Learn <u>in detail</u> all about what Christian Government is!

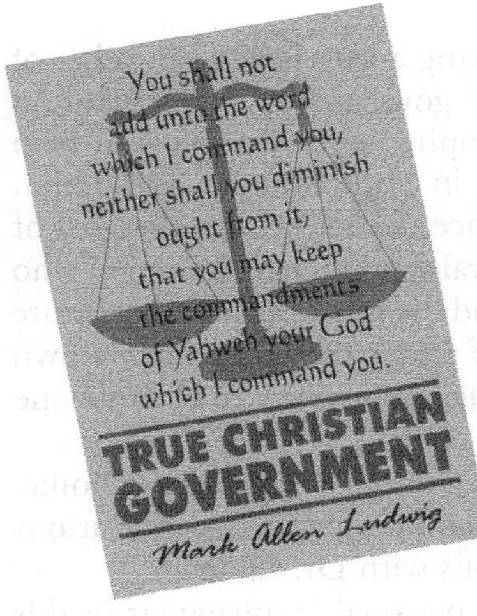

Dr. Ludwig's latest book, *True Christian Government* is the perfect complement to *The Christian Revolutionary.* In it, you will learn exactly what kind of government God intended for mankind to have.

What are the implications of a proper understanding of Adam's sin and of pivotal scriptures about not adding to or taking away from God's law? Here you will find out the big picture. How could such a government be organized? What would the laws be? How would criminals be punished? All of these questions and more are answered in these pages, with plenty of detailed references to the scripture and discussions of what it means. This is the perfect book for the Christian revolutionary who needs a clear vision for a better world!

Please send me _____copies of *The Christian Revolutionary.* I enclose $15 each (cash or check).

Name ________________________________
Address ______________________________

____

____

Send this coupon to:

ARE YOU READY TO GET SERIOUS??

Author Mark Ludwig is offering a very limited number of people the opportunity to study government and revolution with him in depth. He is developing several courses to help people get the solid foundation in both thought and action needed to make a lasting difference in this world. The goal of these materials is, simply put, to raise up men and women who understand their times and can lead the way to a Christian future when the modern state collapses under the weight of its own bankrupt philosophy. This is your opportunity to become one of those knowledgable leaders.

These courses, which you can complete in your own home, include printed course materials, audio tapes, books by various authors, and personal consultations with Dr. Ludwig.

Due to Dr. Ludwig's careful personal involvement in this program, it can only be offered to a very limited number of people at this time.

If you are interested in this program please write requesting full details and an application form. Send all inquiries to:

Dr. Mark Ludwig
c/o Lexington and Concord Partners, Ltd.
P.O. Box 5106
Balboa, Ancon
Panama City 800, Panama

Please make sure to include the proper international postage on your letter.

Get A Free Newsletter from author Mark Ludwig!

Dr. Ludwig publishes a quarterly newsletter, *God and Country*, that is available for free to anyone who would like it. In it, he discusses matters relevant to government, answers questions and shares about his work.

To get a free subscription, simply fill out the coupon below and mail it! (And if you want to send a contribution to cover the expenses of publishing it and our other materials, it will be thankfully received and put to good use!)

☐ **Yes, please send me a free subscription to your newsletter, *God and Country*.**

☐ **Please send information on how I can make money selling these books!**

Name ______________________________

Address ______________________________

____

____

Send this coupon to:

Lexington and Concord Partners, Ltd.
P.O. Box 5106
Balboa, Ancon
Panama City 800, Panama
(Please make sure to include the proper international postage on your letter.)